PRAISE FOR:

Experiential Learning: A Treatise on Education

"We take education for granted, as if we knew what we were doing, but the immense changes in technology, the economy, and our social structure demand that we rethink this essential enterprise with all the creativity we can muster. Our goal is to prepare young people for the opportunities and severe challenges of the mid twenty-first century. Brian Facemire has been devoted to experiential learning for more than a dozen years, all over the globe. The path forward is to rethink education with boldness and creativity, which is just what Brian Facemire has done in his *Treatise on Education*. This remarkable book is Brian's attempt to reform our educational practices to make them equal to the great promise of America. Anyone who cares about the future of education in America will be enlightened and inspired by this book."

—Clay Jenkinson, Host of the Thomas Jefferson Hour

"Brian Facemire walks the talk! *Experiential Learning* is not a dry, didactic book on pedagogy. Instead, Facemire takes us on an experiential learning journey. Through detailed, sensory-rich narratives of his travels and cultural encounters, he demonstrates that learning is about relationships and experience. . . .

"Reading his vignettes . . . I am reminded that experiential learning is embodied cognition, the idea that bodily and sensory interactions with the world shape our thinking. I am reminded that experiential learning is empathy-based learning and is powerful in fostering global citizenship. As such, *Experiential Learning* is a timely call to action for more authentic engagement during this peri-pandemic era in which education has become characterized by less connection, more distanced learning, more technology, and less real-time embodied experience. . . .

"While his expertise as a pedagogical researcher and historian is robust, it is his experience as a teacher, learner, and human being which will inspire readers to practice experiential learning. This book is a must-read for anyone engaged in guiding learning, and most especially for those who are passionate about cultivating lifelong learners."

—Meredith Banasiak, Health Experience Designer and Researcher, Former Faculty University of Colorado

"Facemire is a seasoned educator, thinker, and experiential education advocate. He unapologetically shares his experience, research, and insight into what education can and should be: an experience for the whole human. His book serves as a manifesto, a creed, an inspiration to educators globally and a call to action for the world to view and change educational practices to better suit humans as thinkers, innovators, and integral components of a functioning society. He seamlessly blends and balances journal-style writing with research-supported ideas and personal experience with these practices. Take an experiential journey with Brian and learn what it means to create experiences for learners of all ages and how it positively impacts and propels educational practices beyond mundane, day-to-day tasks to relevant and impactful experiences."

—Becky Schnekser, Educator, Speaker, Author of *Expedition Science: Empowering Learners through Exploration*

"Brian Facemire's *Experiential Learning: A Treatise on Education* is spot on regarding the importance of experiential education in helping prepare students for a fast-changing global world where the age-old practice of traditional education is outdated and ineffective. Facemire's focus on travel as the primary method of experiential education is a deep dive into the benefits of travel in not only creating more awareness and understanding of other cultures but also in character development and spiritual awakening."

—William G. Fluharty, Director of Strategy and Innovation, Cape Henry Collegiate

"As an educator, father of a school-aged child, and a veteran program leader on over a decade of international experiential education adventures with students, Facemire passionately writes his treatise on a topic that we should all be considering when it comes to the current state of educational practices.

"His approach is funny, relevant, relatable, thought-provoking, and frankly, it left me feeling a little sad. It is a reminder that educators have pointed out the benefits of experiential learning for over a hundred years, yet society continues to press on with stagnant educational practices. The book will hopefully leave you questioning your academic perspectives and practices and inspire educators to find ways to provide more experiential education experiences to students of all ages."

—Kim Johnson, Tropical Ecology Field Research
Program Leader, Marine Biology Teacher

"With a critical view of where current schooling is taking us, the book offers an alternative path: to leave traditional teaching spaces behind and to go out and name the world as our classroom. In this text, the strongest case for experiential education comes through stories of the author's lived experiences of traveling globally with his students. In those faraway places, the potential for authentic learning is realized!"

—Chris Garran, Head of School
Cape Henry Collegiate

"Experiential teaching and learning is essential to engage the modern learner. Facemire's lens on teaching today's student versus the one who couldn't readily access content illustrates the changes needed for traditional models of education. His personal experiences leading students to implement what has been debated in the classroom setting and apply it in the field reinforces why students seek him out as a teacher and mentor."

—Brooke Hummel, Assistant Head of School,
Cape Henry Collegiate

Experiential Learning: A Treatise on Education

by Brian A. Facemire

ISBN 978-1-64663-712-6

Published by

köehlerbooks™

3705 Shore Drive
Virginia Beach, VA 23455
800-435-4811
www.koehlerbooks.com

EXPERIENTIAL LEARNING

A Treatise on Education

BRIAN A. FACEMIRE

VIRGINIA BEACH
CAPE CHARLES

This book is dedicated to my beautiful and immensely patient wife, Alisyn, and my young son, Daniel—may you ever seek the truth.

To my students, fortune favors the bold.

TABLE OF CONTENTS

PROLOGUE

I have a masters in secondary education. I wrote my dissertation and conducted my primary research on student perceptions of the benefits of experiential education. That, coupled with fourteen years leading experiential education opportunities all over the globe as well as in my own proverbial backyard, has led me to the conclusions offered here. My own research in 2013 greatly informs the ultimate goal of this book: a call to parents, educators, administrators, and policy makers to destroy the old systems of education and create something based on experiential education that will prepare students for the jobs of the future. (Directions for further research and word-for-word student responses to the open-ended research question that was part of the survey can be found near the end of the book.)

How so? Through experiential education models that can help foster the creative thinkers and circular thought required to lead in this century.

My educational philosophy used to be so technical, so chock-full of the latest edu-speak, that the verbiage sounded more like an educational theory textbook. Education schools make you take classes such as educational theory, followed by some nonsensical series of letters and numbers. It's actually comical. All the theory in the world goes out the

1

window in the first five minutes of your first full-time teaching gig. That is unless you can apply experiential education theory to your programming. You can read all the pedagogical best practices and practical disciplinary theory you want. You may even have a well-thought-out plan for each imaginable scenario, but come day one, what any teacher worth their salt knows is that all that theory doesn't amount to much. Each student comes into the room on a different social, emotional and physical plane. It is not reasonable to conclude that learning to deal with each of these students within their own plane of existence can come from a textbook. It can only come from sincere reflection on past mistakes and experience.

I was so idealistic; I wasn't going to be the proverbial sage on the stage. My classes were going to have discussions—meaningful, deep discussions. What good teachers automatically know and what bad teachers never figure out (they have problems with honest self-reflection, more on that later) is that teaching isn't about pedagogy, discipline, content, or curriculum; it's about relationships and experience. Not like "I know my way around the school" experience but like "I've been changed for the better for having that experience" kind of experience. The incorporation of this type of learning will go a long way toward solving so many of our current societal and cultural problems.

Over the years, my educational philosophy has changed and morphed, as it should. Anybody who thinks the same way they did even a few years ago has a problem with the concept of serious self-reflection (i.e., middling teachers). Nevertheless, my philosophies changed. I'm an avid proponent of experiential education over the usual rows and columns of desks. I'll be the first to admit that it's not perfect—no system is—but it offers the best opportunity for a young person to grow and to have enriching and beneficial experiences that will open their hearts and minds to their passions.

The academic and intellectual origins of this experiential movement are discussed later in the book along with journal-type entries of my own experiences leading international experiential learning opportunities. This authentic experience, though, doesn't exist to the extent that it should in modern schools. In fact, it probably can't realistically exist, on a day-to-day basis and in its purest form, in a school.

Or can it?

The authentic experience is found partly in the relationship. Relationships are the key to creating the authentic experience. Right? Right. As the manuscript moves along, you will find that I offer various answers. But that's not the point. Ever the teacher, I simply wish to engage you well enough that you begin to ask the correct questions. What follows is part philosophy, part academic study, part hourly teaching journal, part dark-education-comedy (the kind that makes you laugh but isn't funny). Down deep in the human soul, it's not funny at all; it's deeply sad and frustrating, and I hope it makes you angry.

You see, I'm admittedly a bit of a rabble-rouser, a malcontent, they say, and a nonconformist. I ask penetrating and tough questions of policies I do not agree with, sometimes publicly, sometimes not. I try to point out the holes in programs that I think could be improved upon and wonder if they have been thought all the way through. I speak loudly, not particularly concerned with who hears me, about the critical areas where schools are failing students. I criticize the administrators who create these programs without the proper input and insight with equal veracity.

I am fortunate to work at a school that tries very hard to be innovative in how we educate our students. My school has a top-class experiential learning program and has recently revealed plans for a state-of-the-art innovation center. This is the type of forward thinking that I would love to see expanded upon further. Those of us who believe strongly in experiential learning are sometimes at odds with those traditional educators who are perhaps less inclined to want their students out of their classrooms on a regular basis. This can be addressed through the creative design of the workspaces that students have access to. The building structures and architecture (discussed in more detail in part V) can help to create a space for internal experiential learning opportunities.

PART I

A Day in the Life of a Fairly Bored Government Teacher

6-ish a.m.

I hit the snooze four or five times. The alarm went off at 5:30 a.m. It goes off at that time every single day, except the weekends. I crawl out of bed and make coffee (it's from Thailand). I'm married, I'm forty, and I teach high school—mostly junior government students but really whoever walks through the door. I have a hard time getting excited even though the 2020 election cycle looms large. Hope we don't get coronavirus.

My mind wanders to closed schools and universities. I wonder how it is going. I shower. I probably linger longer than necessary, but who's counting? Shower thoughts are funny; you end up thinking of the weirdest stuff in there. I dry off and get changed and then sit down at my desk. I have a wonderful spot to work at home, but my desk is mostly for my own pleasure. There are books, pairs of glasses, animal bones, various fossils, and watches I wear sometimes. I like to explore new places and find things that nature discarded many eons ago (or last week, even).

Today, I search for jobs . . . again. I have been rejected by close to a dozen different employers in recent months. There are no jobs relevant to my current level of experience. The problem is, as I see it, that when you're forty years old and you've been stuck in the same career for thirteen years (for example, teaching government), you have no other valuable work experience. At least that's what potential employers see. I look for mostly adjunct positions in education. This makes sense because my master's degree is in education. What doesn't make sense is why I got a master's degree in education. I have always felt that I should have pursued a history degree. I am now engaged in an MA program in the Classical Mediterranean. The universe may never reveal this bit of irony to me, or maybe it does every day and I'm too blind to see it. Somewhere I zigged when I should have zagged.

7:10-ish a.m.

I woke up my son at 7:10-ish. Whatever. I let him sleep in ten extra minutes because of daylight savings time. Breakfast was good this morning. It was simple—granola with milk and two hard-boiled eggs. I ate mine alone before he joined me. He always gets in bed with my wife and dog for a few minutes. It's okay. We won't be late today—not like yesterday when he had to walk straight down to his classroom instead of going into the holding pen, I mean, the cafeteria. We walk to school together every day. These are the good moments, the moments in life that provide that little piece of serenity that gets you through the parts of your day when you feel trapped, exposed, and inadequate.

8:15-ish a.m.

I go back to my classroom. My advisory group is waiting. Some students show up, some do not, but all are required to. No ramifications, no consequences, and no accountability. Another holding pen, only they've learned to escape as they've gotten older and wiser. They go off to class, or somewhere else.

8:20 a.m.

My first bell comes in, US Government and Politics. They're good kids, but many of them don't care about American government. There is no better time to be teaching American government, no moment more interesting than to teach government during a presidential election year. Yet they do not seem the slightest bit interested. I ask myself why that might be. Am I too old to recognize their shared apathy to a system that excludes them?

I teach on. Electoral college and primaries and caucuses . . . oh my! The level of excitement is only surpassed by the alleged sight of a single snow flurry. After gathering the collective mind that has been lost in those few seconds after the completely inappropriate timing of the very public and dramatic announcement of the single snow flurry. I teach on.

I begin the next section with a question regarding a previous election year. Who gets nominated? Bill Clinton played the saxophone, a detail cool enough to lock up the under-thirty vote. My students think it's incredibly not cool. You see, they don't actually care about the snow any more than they care about Bill Clinton; what they crave, and therefore what they care about, is the experience and adventure that the coming of the snow implies. They stare out the window for this reason, their senses immersed in thoughts of future experiences.

9:15 a.m.

The class ends uneventfully, and I have a planning bell. They move on to another class like cogs in a broken machine—into the void beyond. They take their time; some of them will be late to the next class, not necessarily interested in that one either. Of course, there are outliers, anomalies, students who are self-starters, creative thinkers, who are wired differently.

The system is built for so much less than they are or can be. The education system is junk. It is based on a late nineteenth-century industrial model where you shove a piece in one door and other pieces are added to it until you have a complete product, and then it gets shoved out another door. There are usually only a few students who succeed in recognizing this pattern of industrialized brainwashing (disguised as education). Those who do don't have a choice to change it, and the voices of both students and faculty who dare to rise against this dull existence are often considered "difficult." In addition to all this, we claim to be educating students for jobs that likely do not exist yet. The hubris of attempting this within the current system shows clearly that a new system is required. We need a system that delivers to students the tools they will need to navigate within a globalized world. The specter of increasing nationalism on a global scale is a legitimate threat to globalization, but the implementation and immersion of experiential education into our schools can effectively combat this phenomenon as well as provide them with the tools they will need to navigate a globalized world.

Nationalism is historically the strongest 'ism' that impacts global events. Look no further than the revolutions that rocked Europe in 1848. This remains the largest wave of revolutions to occur in Europe, which began shortly after Karl Marx and Friedrich Engels published their Communist Manifesto. This incorrectly led Marx to conclude that these were his predicted uprisings of the proletariat. In fact, these were nationalist revolutions against the conglomerate European empires of the period. Marx spent the rest of his life studying capitalism and eventually published *Das Kapital* in 1867, his definitive critique of the capitalist system. Frankly, nationalism may have met its match in globalism. Time will tell.

This is our education system. How else could it be done? So many ask the question, how do we deliver the tools for jobs that don't exist yet?

Bachelor's degrees are like high school degrees were thirty-five years ago—everyone has one. Any student of primary economics knows that scarcity creates value; it is why diamonds are expensive despite how incredibly common they really are. Diamond companies control the supply in the market and thereby create fake scarcity to drive up the commodity's value. Bachelor's degrees are also incredibly common, yet at this point, there is not an organization available to control the supply in the market. Therefore, the market is flooded with people with bachelor's degrees, making them far less valuable than they once were.

Don't get me wrong; I enjoy living in an educated society, and I do believe people should attend university and be life-long learners, but the system by which we allegedly educate these young people is a system designed to eliminate choice. When you eliminate choice, when you eliminate specialization, you water down the potential creative output of a generation of young people. At this point, since the industrialization in the mid to late nineteenth century, we have watered down no fewer than four generations of American students. Stick that in your vape pen and smoke it.

10:25 a.m.

My third bell arrives. Freshmen take World History II. Basically, this covers the late nineteenth century industrial revolution until as close to modern times as we can get. It's a daunting task, to say the least, but not as daunting as AP World History, when I started with humans migrating out of Africa and ended in a post-September 11 world. They mostly got fives (the highest score). They were heavily engaged. Why? Because of me? No, because of something that is rare in modern times: intrinsic motivation. They were without a doubt the best group of students I have ever had the pleasure to teach. They brought preparedness and energy and respect to the process.

What's AP? It stands for advanced placement, and it is part of an internationally recognized education program from an organization called College Board. You've heard of them; they're the ones still holding the SAT in March 2020 despite it being in the height of the COVID-19 global pandemic. Yeah, they sound like they really have the best interest of the students in mind. In the interest of full disclosure, I teach AP classes, but this is another mind-boggling example of the ruination of the altruistic virtues of education by an organization that takes advantage of high school students through the promise of college credit. The universities are complicit in this. Students, and more importantly their parents, believe they will not get into college without several AP classes on their transcript. The problem with AP classes, in my experience, is that the curriculum is too inflexible. There is very little time for anything outside the curriculum and too little time, therefore, to incorporate authentic experiential learning opportunities. I can't exactly tell the students that. Or can I? If I did, would they understand, would they *listen* or just *hear*? How deep are they capable of thinking? Are they too indoctrinated by a system that has actually attempted to teach them not to think by the time they get to high school?

The teachers are not trying to teach students not to think; the industrial education system embedded in their soul by this point has created a model or product not ripe for open-minded inquiry. Rather, it breeds a model ripe for mind-numbing followership. The ease of access to information has created a student culture in which each student thinks they are an expert in whatever the topic is for that day, and this has devalued the role of the teacher as the educational expert. The system supersedes the best efforts of teachers in too many cases. The best way to combat this phenomenon is to get the students back out into the world to experience the topics discussed in the standard curriculums. Seeing, hearing, and smelling the poverty is meant to make some think twice about the world and offer a greater perspective lens through which to view the world.

I teach on, discussing one hundred years of relative peace and prosperity between 1815 and 1914. Klemens von Metternich, World War I, trench warfare, trench foot, no man's land, and Italy flip-flopped more times than a politician running for president. They don't get the reference. I laugh at my own joke. I do that. They laughed at me laughing at my own joke. "This is the way," said the Mandalorian. They did not laugh. Verdun, the Somme, the Marne. The slaughter. The Russians ran into battle with no weapons, picking up those of their fallen comrades. The Russians industrialized late, late bloomers, defeated. "It led to the rise of the Bolsheviks," I say. This word sounds like a curse word. Giggles ensue, the focus is lost, and six minutes pass before this tragic turn of events can be corrected and we can get back on course. A course correction. Please don't tell me I have to explain the double meaning. Class ends.

11:20 a.m.

Time for fourth bell US Government. This is not a bad group, on the surface. Many are certainly as disinterested as any of the others. This is the second time today I've taught the same material—so even I'm somewhat disinterested at this point. The mundaneness of it all doesn't escape anyone. I take a deep breath, find some professionalism buried deep inside my psyche, and embark on the same journey as before. I hope no one notices my boredom—but of course, they do. "It's a presidential election year," I say. Some acknowledge with a nod. I ramble on about the current state of the Democratic party's primary process and some heads perk up because they've heard the names before, probably from their parents. Sir Thomas Browne called it "the iniquity of oblivion."

12:20 p.m.

It's time for lunch. We dismiss a few minutes early. Everyone is hungry but no one wants to eat. We head to yet another mass holding pen for approximately twenty-five minutes of lunch. The kids complain about the food; it's not Chick-fil-A. It's good food for institutionalized food. There's a salad bar, probably the best bet, and I eat the chicken nuggets. Sodium abounds.

We all gobble down the food as fast as possible like famished Spinosauri. The kids are so programmed to move rapidly through their schedule and are so eager to get on with the next mini version of autocratic rule that they literally line up inside the cafeteria until they can leave. They exit some ten minutes before lunch ends, fifteen minutes before the next class starts. Then the cafeteria is nearly empty; teachers remain for few minutes longer, attempting to gather their sanity, enjoying a mundane yet adult conversation before retuning back to work.

12:55 p.m.

It's 12:55 p.m., time for fifth bell, US Government. Some of them are waiting for me in the classroom. Others are lingering in the hall just outside and hurry in when they see me coming. Some stay outside despite noticing my arrival. Others will be late. Why are they late? They've had fifteen minutes to get there. It certainly wasn't because they went to their locker. I know this because five minutes into class one of them has to go to their locker to get the materials they need to complete the work we are doing in class. Ya know, their government book . . . and their binder, the thing that holds all their notes.

This class is my largest government class and contains my most difficult students. You remember the previous conversation about difficult students? This is them, the ones who aren't particularly interested in school. They seem to innately understand that this particular system isn't for them. It's not that they don't want to be successful students; they do. It's that the system they're in doesn't work for them. They want to care about the electoral college, and they want to care about checks and balances and the current constitutional crisis. But they can't. They've been sold a bill of goods.

Everyone who's ever been to school thinks they're an expert on school. They think they've got it figured out. They don't and they haven't. Well, I take that back. They may understand school, but they don't understand kids. We see kids produced by the current industrial model of education who present themselves as entitled and vainglorious. They didn't start that way; they were created by a system that has proven itself incapable of adapting to their unique set of strengths and skills. They have been failed. Their spirit has been vexed. It's not their fault; it's the system's. So what's the answer? Experiential learning and educational opportunities that allow these students and indeed all students to see, touch and feel these things for extended periods. For example, if we can't go to the Democratic or Republican National Conventions, we need to find ways to recreate that experience.

2:05 p.m.

At 2:05 p.m., and my sixth bell study hall shuffles in. They are juniors, which means they can check out of study hall, relocate within the school, and study somewhere else (or not study somewhere else). Three students of the twelve or fifteen stay each day. Study hall is supposed to be an opportunity for the students to work on their assignments, giving me time to catch up on my work. They generally don't do assignments, and I generally try to work but am easily distracted. Instead, we talk—about various topics, from the merits of modern screamo music to the fact that there are no merits to modern screamo music. We talk about live streaming, rock climbing, and summer jobs. This is truly what study hall was meant for, relationship building. It's not for busywork assignments, and it's not for grading that stack of essays that were turned in a while ago; it's for building relationships with kids. I try to create an experience that is interesting to them and is about them. It's one of the better parts of my day.

We never have all seven bells in one day, so I don't have my AP Comparative Government class today. That class is my largest. How did such a huge percentage of the senior class end up in an AP course? Seriously, I want to know the numbers. It seems ridiculous, with hints of grade inflation and watered-down content. Repetition hones the blade sharp—same as the mind. Skills instruction complete.

There are students in my class who shouldn't be there. I recommended them for the class last year before I knew I was teaching this class this year. I always err on the side of giving kids a chance to take an advanced class. This policy appears to have backfired, and that's okay. I've offered them an experience they may not have ever received before. The kids who shouldn't be there know it. I don't mince words with them; they're seniors, after all, with enough self-awareness to realize it without my saying it. It's a bit funny, and we all muster a laugh, but it's probably not all that funny to them. I shake it off in the moment and think about it at 3 a.m. when I'm wide-awake and wondering to myself. At 3 a.m., my mind flows like Gertrude Stein's stream of consciousness.

Seventh bell AP Comparative Government and Politics is overall a great group of students, all of whom I taught when they were freshmen in my world history course. They know me, I know them, and we all know what to expect. I bore them with my presentations as I fumble and mumble my way through my presentations. It's my first year teaching this course, so I tell myself I'm learning alongside them, but that doesn't seem fair to them. I heard somewhere that fortune favors the prepared mind. They're great kids, though, and I really enjoy our conversations, the ones irrelevant to the course content. That's where I thrive and where I build the relationships necessary to maintain their attention and respect long enough to get through another boring, mind-numbing presentation. I will find a new and better way to teach this course next year.

There will come a time when the old lines in their faces crinkle into a smile and they remember their younger years, and it won't be the moments in dull classrooms sitting in rows and columns that come streaming back; it will be the meaningful experiences we, as teachers, were able to give them.

10:40 p.m.

I'm trying to read fifty-seven pages on epigraphy in the classical world for a second master's degree and my mind won't stop wandering—wandering to COVID-19 and remote learning, wandering to the southwest United States, wandering to the south of Europe, to the north of Europe, wandering to boats and dreaming of small yachts (nothing ostentatious), wandering to archaeological digs that only take place in my mind (like some reckless admiration for the romanticism of the late nineteenth century colonial theft of indigenous artifacts).

My spirit is restless. I'm bored. I need new adventure. I crave new scenarios, new parks, new people, new ways of life, new innovative and creative spaces to engage students in new ways. I work in a place where these creative spaces are coming to life and there is freedom to explore new experiences for both students and educators alike. But if I feel this way, imagine how the students feel, and imagine how teachers and students feel who are not afforded the opportunities that myself and my students have at our fingertips. I'm bored—but *never* bored of the students. Relationships can be the experience when the rest of life seems mundane. The measure of a good teacher isn't AP exam test scores; it's how they're remembered by their students that counts. People don't remember theorems or historiography; they remember the people who made those things interesting, who offered them an opportunity to choose to be a part of the learning process, and who held them accountable for that choice.

PART II

Remote Learning and the System that Kills Us

I went fishing—for jobs—and there were no bites. If I were actually fishing, this experience would be the equivalent to my bait getting snatched by crabs every time I cast the line out. It is the middle of a global pandemic; of course, no one is hiring. Remote learning saved my career, at least for the time being. It gave me time to reflect, to be human, and to take care of myself.

I'm savvy enough to understand the opportunity the COVID-19 quarantine presented to us all. It gave us all a moment in time to reflect on what's important. As a society, so many seem to have missed the opportunity. In the race to open the economy, riots ravaged cities on a global scale in the summer of 2020, and social media distracted us from the bigger picture.

I used the time to get myself fit—mentally and physically. I was an all-around happier human being, taking more time to care for myself. This realization gave me great pause. I began to ask questions that had previously passed by fleetingly. Now, with time, these questions seemed to hold more weight.

Why do we, in the prime of our lives, give ourselves to a system that slowly kills us, breaks us, and stresses us?

We are constantly connected to problems at work through our devices. The social media feeds are endless; there is no end of the chapter, no logical stopping point built into the system. That's why you could waste four hours of your day staring at a screen and not even know it. The constant and addictive technological connectivity creates a self-defeating system of comparisons with a stranger's curated life. Somewhere in this world, someone is camping in the remote woods, delightfully happy.

Why?

Because that person is disconnected and hasn't been told via social media what they are supposed to be angry and upset about this week. I was so much happier working remotely, with time for my own mental health and physical wellness. So many people harp on the fact that society's mental health is declining as a result of quarantine. While this is certainly true in many cases, I am in the exact opposite position. My mental health apparently thrives in a quarantine situation. It allowed me time to explore this creative outlet (writing a book). The level of teenage angst being exhibited by adults who love to live in the accountability-free zones of social media is astronomically high right now. More time in a disconnected state is crucial for the mental health of our world.

The argument that students are suffering great mental health consequences is a concern, and that carries a lot of weight with me. Students over the years have confided in me their suicidal tendencies, and I have, of course, dealt with those scenarios appropriately. However, the greater concern and tougher question is not the immediate and temporary (ultimately we have returned to in-person instruction) mental health issues created by remote learning; it's why being in quarantine has either created or exacerbated these issues and why many of them have persisted beyond the remote learning experience. It seems to me we have an opportunity to create a more resilient and less entitled society through this experience. Why not use this opportunity to strengthen the mental health of our society, with open communication and acknowledgment of the problems that face our collective society? Many of these problems seem directly linked to social media's hold over our lives.

We shouldn't be surprised by the system that we are all embroiled in today; it is the exact economic and political system that the education system prepared us for. But that preparation was filled with false promises dictated by false prophets. These false prophets included our parents, our teachers, our community, and religious leaders.

The most prominent lie our society tells is that you can "be anything you want if you work hard." You can be anything you want—as long as you have the money and privilege needed to get there. While money may not equal happiness, it certainly equals freedom and stability. And freedom plus stability equals happiness—the happiness to choose the path that's right for you, the path that offers the best level of mental health, the path that sets your soul ablaze with passion, and the path that allows you to do the things that you feel you were meant to do. What I've noticed over the years is that those with the financial stability to do so will often times choose some type of artistic endeavor, rather than being forced to sell their soul working in a job they hate in order to the pay the mortgage. Experiential education initiatives for all ages of learners can save people from this fate.

What do I mean by this?

I mean that the essence of the human soul is not meant to be caged in cubicles and brick-and-mortar buildings. Some people, even with all that freedom, may still choose something corporate or traditional, and that's okay. But for those who have no choice, for those who are forced to endure these horrid, stressful, and unhappy conditions for any length of time, for those whose souls aren't meant for these paths, we must fight to eliminate these conditions from our lives. This question is the most distressing because there is no answer. Often times, even if the answer is found, those without financial means simply cannot achieve their soul's goals. They become stuck in their comfort zone. And just like that, the dream is dead on arrival. Shame on them for falling for it, for believing it could happen.

But why is it dead?

The dream began to die long before modern times, though it has ebbed and flowed and has experienced resurgences. This mostly occurs in times of great crisis, during those rare moments where the American people united around a common goal, often a common enemy. The education system is based on a nineteenth century industrial model. Compulsory education was created during this period of the second industrial revolution because the government needed to intervene in a system incapable of regulating itself. It turns out that nine-year-old kids shouldn't be working in industrial factories without even the slightest safety regulations. Even with the safety regulations, it's probably best to skip the nine-year-olds.

The government had to step in and place regulations on industrialists, implementing rules within the whole system that would ensure workers were taken care of. It was originally believed that the industrialist market would take care of this on their own, reinvesting their profits back into safer equipment and into the well-being of their workers. This clearly didn't happen on a large scale, not enough to make a difference to the vast majority of industrial factory workers. Imagine factory owners lounging in their gilded regality, almost emperor-like in their gluttony for material wealth. Juxtapose that image with a factory worker in poor working conditions.

In 1911, the Triangle Shirtwaist Factory fire, killed 145 women; the exits were locked due to fear of theft of materials by the employees. And this is just one large-scale example; there were countless maims and deaths on a smaller and individualized scale. People, human beings, were dying, and the industrialists did very little to address the problem. The government was forced—yes, forced—to step in and create regulations that protected the workers. This protection has evolved over time and become more sophisticated, as it should, but the point is, people had to die. Once the money started flowing, the industrialists were incredibly reluctant to give up a single dime for the people who worked those dangerous, dusty, and oftentimes disease-infested factory floors.

Compulsory education wasn't introduced during this period by the government for altruistic reasons, "to ameliorate the condition of mankind" as Thomas Jefferson so eloquently put it; rather, it was created to protect children from factory work and thereby provide more opportunities for adults to have gainful employment. Improving literacy rates was a priority, though this was not because we needed to live in a more educated society; it was because the capitalists could not be trusted to do the right thing and appropriately take proper care of their workers. The system was purposely rigged against the workers, and arguably still is. Again, I argue that experiential education is the answer. Building global thought processes through immersion in foreign cultures has the potential to result in greater empathy for all.

I read that, in 2021, the technology company Apple surpassed $2 trillion dollars in net worth. Apple has historically been considered a progressive company, present at the conception and birth of the Northern California Silicon Valley culture. But are they really? I'm certain they give millions to charities on a global scale, but could that wealth be redistributed to those most in need, to mitigate the root causes of world hunger, ranging from war, disease, and agricultural pests to economic factors such as falling crop prices or rising food costs? Imagine what could be accomplished with two trillion dollars. Imagine the number of people who might be able to use this food to nourish themselves and their families. Imagine the cure for cancer or an infectious disease. Imagine all we could do if we simply nourished people in a different way, encouraged them to pursue their passions, and approached education experientially.

Estimates vary widely with regard to the cost of ending world hunger. According to a report published in 2016 by the International Institute for Sustainable Development, that cost is an extra $11 billion per year until 2030. The authors, David Laborde, Livia Bizikova, Tess Lallemant, and Carin Smaller, suggest that money will be divided between public spending within developing countries and donors. This is a worthwhile goal and seemingly achievable within the next decade.

What could be done with $2 trillion dollars? I am completely aware that this money is not necessarily located in a vault somewhere within the depths of Apple's design studios in California, nor in its assembly factories in China; rather, it is spread across thousands of investors all over the world. But, with the proper policies in place, Apple and perhaps a cohort of their tech giant brethren could theoretically invest in ending world hunger in the next ten years. But they won't. And the reason they won't is the exact same reason that the industrialists were incapable and unwilling to regulate themselves—greed.

What a rigged system.

So, how do we fix this system? And how do we prepare students for jobs that do not yet exist?

Experiential education.

PART III

Philosophical Foundations of Experiential Learning

W as humankind really meant to experience this life in a cubicle or at a desk (or whatever the perceived prison is)? We should be out experiencing this world. For all its faults and negative aspects, there is a sunset, a rainbow, a flower, an ocean, or a mountain that, when you look at it, makes you feel alive. Observing these simple pleasures in life happens too rarely for students, teachers, and everyone, really. We're trapped in a place that rips our souls to shreds and our humanity to bits, allowing us no time to be bold or breathe in the air just to taste it. One has to throw off the shackles, get out into the world, see things, smell things, and taste other cultures. Eat what they eat, sleep where they sleep, and live among other people. This eliminates divisiveness once it becomes apparent that most people in the world are simply going about their daily lives wanting the same things as everyone else: a better life for themselves and their children. Incorporation of this type of experiential education into every student's curriculum is necessary to prepare them for the globalized world. The world is a vast place, and cultures might appear vastly different, but our goals are intricately connected.

Widely considered to be the greatest rock climber of his generation and perhaps ever, Alex Honnold once stated, "Nobody achieves anything great being happy and cozy." Alex lives his life pushing the edge further out. He, to date, is the only human to ever free solo the greatest granite wall on planet earth, El Capitan in Yosemite National Park.

Free soloing—for those of you living under the rock, not climbing it—is when a climber attempts to climb a massive slab of rock, like granite or sandstone (or something else entirely, depending on the part of the world they're in), without the security of ropes.

For some perspective, El Capitan is roughly 3,600 feet or 1,100 meters (about twice the height of the Empire State Building) above the floor of Yosemite Valley. For some perspective, that's the equivalent of approximately eighty school buses stacked on top of each other end to end. Now, I'm not suggesting we all need to go out and free solo; most of us would probably die. But we do all need more experiences that make us feel the euphoria that our human souls crave, that feeling that is present on Alex Honnold's face and in his eyes when he "tops out" (when a climber pulls themselves over the ledge at the top). We need to be more comfortable being uncomfortable. It's out on that edge where you experience what life is meant to feel like.

Whatever your edge is, find it and push it and learn what the air tastes like out there. It's different out on that edge, wherever your edge is, it feels different, that's because your soul has been set ablaze with passion for it. Experiential education offers the opportunity to discover these passions.

History of Experiential Education

Jean Batten, an aviator from New Zealand, in her book *Alone in the Sky* wrote, "Every flyer who ventures across oceans to distant lands is a potential explorer; in his or her breast burns the same fire that urged the adventurers of old to set forth in their sailing-ships for foreign lands." Neither students nor their educators are immune to this fire. In fact, educators across the globe are trying to provide unique experiential learning opportunities for their students.

The philosophical foundations of experiential learning are extensive and there have been many contributors to this line of educational thought. There have, however, been three contributors considered to be the most influential in developing the philosophy behind experiential learning theory. Those men are John Dewey, Jean Piaget, and Kurt Lewin. Some consider David A. Kolb to be a major contributor as well, though much of his work is based on a combination of the previous three educational philosophers. Kolb does, however, add a substantial amount of insight to the literature and will be considered often in the following analysis.

John Dewey was an educational philosopher active during the first half of the twentieth century. His theories on experiential learning come from his experiences within the newly minted progressive schools of the era. In short, his experiences developed and changed his perceptions of his own previous theories on education. Dewey forms his philosophy quite simply in his work from 1938, *Experience & Education*, not in terms of traditional versus progressive education models but rather ". . . what anything whatever must be to be worthy of the name *education*" (Dewey 1938, 90). In order to fully understand Dewey's remarks, we must, however, engage in the defining of two terms: traditional education and progressive education. Dewey writes on traditional education,

> If the underlying ideas of the former are formulated broadly . . . The subject-matter of education consists of bodies of information and of skills that have been worked out in the past; therefore, the chief business of the school is to transmit them to the new generation. In the past, there have also been developed standards and rules of conduct; moral training consists in forming habits of action in the conformity with these rules and standards. Finally, the general pattern of school organization

(by which I mean the relations of pupils to one another and to the teachers) constitutes the school a kind of institution sharply marked off from other social institutions (Dewey 1938, 17).

Randolph S. Bourne provides validation to Dewey's critiques of this traditional education model in his essay "In a Schoolroom" in *The New Republic* from November 7, 1914. He writes,

> For the whole machinery of the classroom was dependent evidently upon this segregation. Here were these thirty children, all more or less acquainted, and so congenial and sympathetic that the slightest touch threw them all together into a solid mass of attention and feeling. Yet they were forced, in accordance with some principle of order, to sit at these stiff little desks, equidistantly apart, and prevented under penalty from communicating with each other. All the lines between them were supposed to be broken. Each existed for the teacher alone. In this incorrigibly social atmosphere, with all the personal influences playing, they were supposed to be, not a network or group, but a collection of things, in relation only with the teacher (Bourne 1914, 10).

In his essay, Bourne is sharply critical of the traditional model of education. His essay is based on his own observations within what he calls a "modern classroom." His observations, even in the early twentieth century, and despite the advent of many more progressive models over the course of the century, are still relevant. Many classrooms still adopt the style described in his lines above. In fact, there are paintings from medieval times that depict classrooms exactly as they are arranged today: rows and columns of discomfort that lack any resemblance to the real world. Experiential education has the potential to fix this.

COVID-19 mitigation strategies in schools that are open to in-person learning have exaggerated this as well. Students are required to stay seated in the desks exactly six feet apart or more. They are prevented from close social interaction. This makes sense in the times of COVID-19, but why has it taken a forced mitigation strategy to show the truth? This model represents more prison than educational institution.

In the early twentieth century, progressivism in schools aimed to change the *status quo*, though there have been varying levels of success. The reality is that the traditional education model is an industrial assembly-line model based on the concept of filing students mundanely and unhappily through one set of doors with the ultimately lofty and worthy goal of producing a finished product and pushing them out another set of doors. Again, we see how COVID mitigation protocols have exaggerated this model into clear view.

Each morning, students line up on designated dots six feet apart in order to enter the school, hand over a screening form, and have their temperature taken. They are then only permitted to go directly to their first class of the day. As I stated earlier, this makes sense in the time of COVID, but it is only now that this exaggerated version of the real school day has brought the industrial model into light. Bourne describes the common scene of students leaving the traditional classroom. He writes,

> The 'good' children straightened up, threw off their depression and took back their self-respect, the 'bad' sobered up, threw off their swollen egotism, and prepared to leave behind them their mischievousness in the room that had created it. Everything suddenly became human again. The brakes were off, and life, with all its fascinations of intrigue and amusement, was flowing once more. The school streamed away in personal and intensely interested little groups. The real world of business and stimulations and rebounds was thick again here (Bourne 1914, 12).

Bourne was a critic of the traditional education model, whereas Dewey wanted to define the traditional education model and the progressive model. Here we see again how COVID-19 mitigation protocols have shed light on this issue. Now, during the height of the pandemic, even when students leave their classrooms, they cannot congregate in social groups, and they must go directly to their next little prison cell. This was largely a useless protocol, then and now (but we were not to know that as the pandemic surged). As Bourne describes, during that time, the little groups immediately and automatically formed and huddled, ebbed and flowed, discussing the happenings of the day. In some schools in the 2020-2021 period, there were one-way hallways designated with the same yellow and black arrows one might find on a factory floor.

Dewey believed not in the juxtaposition of these two models but the idea that a properly formed theory of experience could be included in the model. Dewey does, however, go on to sharply criticize the model of the progressive schools. He writes,

> Yet I am sure that you will appreciate what is meant when I say that many of the newer schools tend to make little or nothing of organized subject-matter of study; to proceed as if any form of direction and guidance by adults were an invasion of individual freedom, and as if the idea that education should be concerned with the present and future meant that acquaintance with the past has little or no role to play in education (Dewey 1938, 22).

Dewey exaggerates, but he makes a valid point. Some of the progressive schools aimed to eliminate all forms of the traditional model of education. This presents several problems, the first of which is organization. Any student of childhood development will attest to the fact that in order for children to reach certain developmental milestones there must be a legitimate level of organization and order available within the constructs of their educational curriculum. If experience is to truly become part of a viable educational theory, then, as Dewey points out, educators must answer the question, "What is the place and meaning of subject matter and of organization *within* experience?" (Dewey 1938, 20).

The question is certainly still relevant in today's world. How should educators approach this question? The experience should be preceded by relevant subject matter as it relates to the experience. The subject matter should be embedded in the experience, and then time should be made for reflection on the experience as it relates to not only the subject matter but also to the growth of the individual. This should be the curriculum cycle.

With all this organization—many times based on either outdated curriculum or the latest and greatest buzzword of edu-speak, never on the current moment, never on the current state of a student's life—the question becomes, does this truly constitute an authentic experience? Does the authenticity lie in a certain lack of organization?

I believe it does. Not all aspects of a student and teacher's relationship require a curriculum. In fact, the more unconventional the curriculum, the better, as that is where you find the authentic and organic conversation, where relationships are built, where life is lived, and where passions emerge with clarity and infectious energy. This is the antithesis of the current industrial system. Where, then, does that leave the dissemination of knowledge? Is the simple dissemination of knowledge an outdated method of instruction? Some say yes; some say no. There is certainly an art to delivering a successful lecture, and I quite enjoy it on occasion.

But Dewey also addresses another clear problem facing the progressive education movement in his work. "Now we have the problem of discovering the connection which actually exists *within* experience between the achievements of the past and the issues of the present" (Dewey 1938, 23).

Educators of history, myself included, are in an extremely unique situation. Every passing day adds to our content area. We must think not only in terms of the past but also how that affects the lives of today's students. We are tasked with making the past relevant right now.

The experiential learning opportunity is crucial in developing the student's ability to make the connection. An educational philosophy simply cannot be a solid, codified, tried, and tested set of ideas; rather, it must be as fluid and dynamic as the emotional state of the students and their individual learning styles and perceptions. In *Experience & Education*, Dewey attempted to establish a legitimate experiential learning theory for the progressives and to define the role of experience in their model—in other words, a theory of educational experience that can be applied in a manner relative to the criteria of educational theory noted above.

Educators engaged in experiential learning anywhere should bear in mind the following problem, especially those educators involved in these types of programs at the secondary education level. Dewey correctly concludes, "The belief that all genuine education comes about through experience does not mean that all experiences are genuinely or equally educative" (Dewey 1938, 25).

The question becomes how to make the experiential learning opportunity genuinely educative each time. Making the experience itself equally educative is problematic; participating students tend to have different perceptions, emotional states, and cognitive development levels. Determining whether the experience was equally educative can become highly subjective.

At the secondary level, educators should focus on creating equal experiential learning opportunities for the students to participate in experiences. Again, the student's own perceptions will not allow for complete educative equality. I've learned over the past fourteen years leading expeditions and experiences all over the world from Yellowstone to Borneo that the appreciation of the experience comes later—rarely does it happen in the moment. As an educator, I am inevitably and indelibly concerned with the future. I have learned not to take the appearance of a lack of gratitude or appreciation of the experience personally. They all come around in the long run when they think back on that seminal program in Morocco or Turkey or Peru or wherever. Hope for the future is what drives me to the next experience, to the next adventure, and to the edge of the proverbial cliff mentioned earlier.

H.G. Wells said, "Civilization is a race between education and catastrophe." Never before, in my lifetime, has this sentiment seemed more apropos. The way to combat the catastrophe is through experience and authentic relationships. No longer can the millennia-old models of education achieve what our society requires. They have to change. For all the negative consequences of the COVID-19 pandemic, the positive must come in the form of honest reflection and a reformation (if not complete upheaval) of societal norms that got us to a place where the republic is endangered; the people tasked with upholding it are tired. We are tired of the damn burdens placed on us by broken systems of education and healthcare and politics and media. We must adopt a new experiential system, one that puts emphasis on authentic relationships, thereby strengthening even our youngest learners. The change seems to be happening organically at all levels of education, at least for those fortunate enough to be learning in person. More nature, more walks, more physical activity embedded in the day, more authentic conversation, and less information dissemination, less regurgitation, and less curriculum-based downtime.

Another argument Dewey articulates is that each experience might be disconnected and therefore not concurrently linked to other experiences. This argument may hold water at the higher-education or adult education level; however, at the secondary level, the philosophy is to moderately connect the experience to the curriculum, encouraging reflection after the experience. In other words, the experiential learning opportunity includes the moderately implemented curriculum, the experience, and the reflection.

John Dewey's goal in *Experience & Education* was not to choose between traditional and progressive education; rather, his goal was to highlight the need for a viable educational theory regarding experiential learning and how experiential learning should be incorporated into the overall concept of a traditional education, indeed, to blend the traditional and the progressive concepts.

Experiential Reflection #1

Over the years, I have led various experiences around the world. In 2013, I was chosen by Ocean Exploration Trust to join the Corps of Exploration and serve as an Educator at Sea; my student was chosen to participate in the honors student program. The students chosen spent some time at the University of Rhode Island working on research projects and then participating in real research with real scientists on board a working research vessel such as the *EV Nautilus*. What follows is told from my perspective leading this experience.

Day 1, August 19, 2013, in Bodrum, Turkey

The city of Bodrum, Turkey, is situated in Southwest Turkey, just south of Knidos on the Datça Peninsula. It is a resort town, the harbor filled with yachts of all types, shapes, and sizes. We are taken from the airport, my two young charges and myself, to our ship, the *STS Bodrum*. Dr. Mike Brennan, the expedition leader, greets us. I am immediately taken aback by his relative youth, and I immediately feel inadequate. He is obviously a driven man with a vastly different life experience than mine thus far; nonetheless, our worlds are pulled together for this experience.

Many of the people I meet are young. Let this not, however, deter from their level of professionalism—though their youthful enthusiasm is apparent and contagious. After a few hours aboard the ship becoming accustomed to our close quarters and getting our sea legs, we head off for dinner. All of the adults associated with the expedition order beers. I, alas, do not, as the school for which I work forbids this while I have young people under my care and supervision. It's not a bad policy; though, at times, it can be difficult to navigate in social environments without a beer. I try to sleep. It's hot, unimaginably, unbearably hot.

Day 2, August 20, 2013, *STS Bodrum*

We have gotten underway at roughly 5 a.m. I awake at nearly 7 a.m. and brush my teeth. At breakfast, I speak with Art Trembanis, a graduate of Duke and William and Mary. He's the head of a team of engineers from the University of Delaware who will run the autonomous underwater vehicle (AUV).

Later in the morning, we have an "all hands" meeting on deck to discuss the process of launching the AUV and how that will be done. I watch closely as the team of engineers ready the AUV for launch. Much of the talk is highly technical jargon with which I am unfamiliar, though it is incredibly interesting. The AUV is successfully launched through a combination of pulleys and cranes on deck that lower the vehicle to a small dingy from which a University of Delaware team member will assist in releasing the vehicle into the water. Its mission will take roughly three hours.

Downtime is spent how you might think. Some people monitor the progress of the AUV while others converse about the topics of the day or write papers; students attempt to complete their summer calculus homework, and archaeologists look at pictures of Ephesus' circles. Just your standard crew conversation.

Lunch is spaghetti and some tzatziki, beans, carrots, and some type of sweet potato dish. The recovery of the AUV was interesting. So, let's look at how the AUV works. It's autonomous, which means it's not tethered to the ship in any way. It is programmed with a specific route, usually on a rectangular grid pattern, with a sonar survey of the ocean floor along its programmed route. On this occasion, the battery was allowed to run all the way down. When this happens, it has to float to the surface from approximately 370 meters down. Its rate of ascension is approximately half a meter per second. You can do the math.

The other issue here is that we are on a sailboat, so maneuverability is a bit problematic. Yet another issue is that we are not quite sure of the exact geographic coordinates of the AUV. We have an approximation of the general location. We followed an all-hands-on-deck procedure, searching the horizon in all directions, and when necessary, used our hands to shield our eyes from the Southern Aegean sun.

Allison Fundis—the Ocean Exploration Trust education-initiative representative on board and the person I had mostly been in communication with during the run-up to the expedition—was the first to spot the AUV floating lazily in the water approximately 140 meters behind the boat. I guess I thought it would be more scientific than that.

The AUV was recovered and brought back onto the ship using the same outriggers mentioned earlier. In order to complete the second AUV mission of the day, we switched out the battery with an identical battery module. To do this, it is necessary to unscrew the setscrew and twist the conical nose counterclockwise and pull it off. The battery module sits behind the nose cone and is a lithium-ion battery. The entire module is replaced with a new one. After this tedious and careful process was complete, we were able to launch the AUV for its second mission of the day. Just a day in the life of field science. Not the worst gig I can think of.

The AUV came back, however, with an issue. The engineer crew, led by Art Trembanis, was getting a signal via their equipment that there was a leak somewhere. In other words, the AUV was getting wet internally. Now, having seen a bit of the insides of this incredibly expensive and delicate piece of equipment, it is completely full of electronics. This is what allows it, obviously, to be programmed and subsequently complete its missions. The situation is a bit tense, bordering on awkward; sometimes the AUV team was at odds with the archaeologists. The reason, it seems to me, is that fieldwork often produces published papers for scientists, outlining the new concepts, theories and discoveries made while spending weeks away. In allowing students to see these professional working relationships, we allow them insight into how to solve problems. This is the answer to the question of how we prepare students for jobs that do not exist. It is not about the specific job, and maybe it never has been; it is about learning to navigate the relationships incorporated into our daily lives. When equipment fails, it puts the chances of this publication in jeopardy, and this creates tension.

Dinner was a traditional Turkish meal consisting of lentil soup and vegetable stew. Often times traditional dishes around the world are the simplest. People use what's available to them and establish cuisine based on these availabilities. On these trips, I always try to listen to the conversations around me. Not eavesdropping, per se, just listening and observing carefully. I overheard that the AUV may be down for a day, possibly even two days. That puts the next few days and perhaps the extent of our stay aboard the ship in question. What will these next few days hold for us?

After dinner Dan, an archaeologist from Luther College in Iowa, gave an excellent presentation on the role of the archaeologist on this expedition. His role along with Tufan Turanli, the Turkish archaeologist, was to interpret the seafloor mapping data in search of any anomalies that could possibly be the site of an ancient shipwreck.

Tufan was an interesting character. He looked sort of like a Turkish Bill Murray. First and foremost, he's a renowned archaeologist. Tufan has been working on nautical archaeological expeditions since 1975, and he has participated in all the major excavations in Turkey since that date—especially on the Uluburun Bronze Age wreck, the world's oldest shipwreck ever excavated, a project he's been involved with for the past eleven years.

Turanli has been excavating the Ottoman Frigate, Ertugrul, off the coast of Japan, since 2004 with his wife, archaeologist Berta Lledo Turanli. He is also the chairman of the BOSAV Foundation of Bodrum, Turkey, dedicated to developing the arts and culture of the city. What an absolute privilege for myself and more importantly for my students to work with and learn from Dr. Turanli and his colleagues on this expedition.

The location where we anchored for the evening—an island we've nicknamed "Two-Tree Island" for obvious reasons—was fairly important in ancient Mediterranean maritime trade. If you close your eyes and think just a little bit, you can transport yourself back in time to the Byzantine era, then back to the time of Homer, and if you squeeze your eyes hard and let go, you may even see the soldiers of Agamemnon sailing these same salty seas. Imagine being anchored off a small island in the southeastern Aegean Sea, the stars as bright and plentiful as you've ever witnessed, the same stars looked upon by Odysseus on his epic journey. This *is* experiential learning.

There was nearly no ambient light, and the climate was cool enough in the evenings to sleep on mattresses outside on the deck. Somewhere from near the bow—you can't be sure who is speaking—someone begins to recite whole sections of Homer's *Iliad*, his lasting epic of the Trojan War, or is it the *Odyssey*? At that moment, it couldn't matter less. These are the moments that allow students the rarest opportunities— opportunities that will help shape their thinking, help them discover their passions, help them determine what sets their soul on fire.

Day 3, August 21, 2013, *STS Bodrum*

The day began with a somber mood on board. The mission had been placed on hold for the time being. The AUV was down due to the water detection sensor that alerted the team to the possibility of a leak. All on boards were a bit idle. Some of the students were reading, doing summer work; some were snorkeling. Everyone else was doing research or writing—and waiting. All of the morning was spent repairing the AUV. The engineers had the entire AUV apart in pieces on the table and they narrowed down the location of the leak.

Val, one of the engineers, had touched a nylon plastic screw and found that he could turn the screw with his finger. This had been analyzed and determined to be the cause of the leak alert. They pieced the machine back together and the AUV was prepared for a test dive. We were hopeful for a dive that afternoon. We didn't want to lose a day.

During part of the morning, I was able to assist in analyzing some of the data from our previous mission dives. Essentially this involved scrolling through what amounts to several kilometers of seafloor sonar imagery in an effort to identify possible anomalies on the seafloor. Ultimately, the archaeologists are looking for clusters of amphorae which is the telltale sign of an ancient shipwreck's location. The wood from the ship will have long since deteriorated and decayed in the oxygen-rich environment, but the ancient version of the modern shipping container, the amphora, will still be intact on the bottom.

The AUV had run several successful tests, one of which nearly ran the machine into the hull of the ship on its return. The debate became whether or not to plan and program a full mission that afternoon.

The mission was attempted; it was not completed. The guys were in the dingy ready to launch the AUV, but the modem wouldn't sync up or align with the AUV, so it was retrieved. The team opted for prudence over valor. It was probably a good idea as our luck did not seem to be changing for the better that day. We would attempt to complete three dives the following day, the first of which would launch before breakfast at 6 a.m.

We had a great night swim and yet another fabulous dinner. Val, one of the AUV engineers, gave a talk about the basics of sonar. It was a smart, highly intellectual affair, well over my head and the heads of my high school kids, but they hung in there. They displayed maturity and professionalism and took what they could from the experience. It was an incredibly humbling experience to be around these people. Their passion and expertise was second to none, and we were lucky to be a part of it.

Day 4, STS Bodrum

Most were up early in anticipation of an early launch for the AUV. The plan was for three dive missions that day to make up the missed time the previous day. It became eerily apparent that we would probably not finish what we came to accomplish. That that fact did not cause more conflict and tension among the interested parties is a testament to their professionalism and perseverance in the face of hardship.

That was the roughest day on the water, pretty choppy. Of course, our calmest day was the day before when we didn't have the AUV in the water. Unfortunately, the AUV came home with another leak warning and our project leaders shut it down again. We had three Turkish scientists on board with us for a day or so, from a tech company in Turkey, who were incredibly interested in the AUV and had been pumping the AUV team (Carter, Val, and Art) with dozens of questions since they arrived. They were presented with the data that has been collected so far. It seemed apparent to me that our sonar mapping mission using the AUV was over.

The day was Thursday, August 22, 2013. We were scheduled to depart our location at 3 p.m. I wasn't sure how the mission would change from then on. It took five hours to sail north by northwest to our anchor spot, arriving around 8 p.m. We took many of the same routes as the ancient mariners, passionately seeking to understand them. Then, we stalled; for about an hour, we only made it one knot, sailing by the island of Kos. Once we rounded the island, our speed picked up to between six and seven knots. That was an incredible experience, my first true sailing experience in which the ship tilted harshly to one side under the strength of the wind. We had an amazing journey, a wonderful sail.

The sunset that evening was exquisite. In fact, I've seen sunsets on four continents, in different climates, but the most striking was in the Aegean Sea just off the coast of Turkey. We slept on the deck that night. The stars were exceptionally bright. Our souls were on fire.

Day 5, STS Bodrum

We were awake for yet another amazing sunrise around 6 a.m. and had breakfast around 7:30 a.m. We sailed into port that morning and went into town in search of snorkel gear. Customs was . . . interesting. We just followed Tufan and Mustafa (the ship captain) straight through, no questions asked. We walked through town a bit and found several closed dive shops and were about to give up when we happened upon a souvenir shop and were able to collect the appropriate gear for snorkeling. We got off cheaper than we would have at any dive shop.

In the afternoon, we split into two groups. One would go ashore the island to explore and the other would snorkel in the crystal clear, blue water. The island where we anchored was called Çavuş Adası. Tufan first did work there back in 2000, before the world changed. We were back because the AUV was down for the count and would not be back in action. It was a disappointment to all on board, but Plan B was in full motion at Çavuş Adası.

There was a large man-made breakwater a few meters below the surface. There were shipwrecks on either side of the island, and if there had been dive gear aboard the ship, I would have explored them. The theory was that both ships sunk because they were overloaded with stone. They were taking the stone from the back side of the island opposite the breakwater and moving it to the other side to create the breakwater. There is still some debate over whether the breakwater was actually above sea level at the time it was built or whether it was always a submerged structure like it is now.

I was on the team that snorkeled first. We found some broken amphorae and hundreds of potsherds. It seemed obvious that the structure is man-made. After dinner, I was lucky enough to go ashore with Dr. Mike Brennan and Dr. Dan Davis. It was very interesting to just walk around and listen to Mike and Dan talk and bounce ideas off each other and hear how the process works for developing theories like the one above.

When we returned, the students gave presentations. They had attended a five-week institute over the summer at the University of Rhode Island where they created their own scientific experiments and presented the results. After three fabulous student presentations, we all sat around the table and debriefed the photographic and physical evidence discovered over the course of the day. It was really impressive to witness this process. I sincerely hope to be a part of something like this someday as an expert in a field, hopefully archaeology. My students and I were fortunate to experience authentic science in real time.

This experience perfectly defines experiential education. The entirety of our education system should be based on this model. Each year of high school should include several of these types of authentic experiences, which brings me to funding.

The Money

The United States currently invests less in public education than its industrialized western counterparts. According to educationdata.org, the international standard for education spending, set by organizations like UNESCO, is approximately 15 percent of a public budget. The United States comes in well below the international standard at approximately 11.6 percent. "Schools in the United States spend an average of $12,612 per pupil, which is the fifth highest amount per pupil among the thirty-seven other developed nations in the Organization of Economic Cooperation and Development" (educationdata.org).

There are really two issues here—the amount spent per pupil and how the funding is spent. I would argue we are spending the money in old-fashioned and inefficient ways. Textbooks and, yes, even iPads and other technology, are no longer adequate. There was a thankfully brief moment in influential educational thinking circles when iPads were going to replace experience as a learning tool. Why fly to Rome to see the Coliseum when you can take a virtual tour? Why learn to sail aboard the *STS Bodrum* in search of ancient civilizations when you can watch it on YouTube? In the times of COVID, we have seen a resurgence of this type of thinking. There is even more emphasis on these devices in education.

I would argue that, while there are educational merits to these devices, that reliance on them to provide an authentic experience is folly. Our school recently invested in several sets of virtual reality goggles, which are very cool and offer a far better experience than that of the iPad travel experience, but nothing can replace the actual experience. The smells, the tastes, the moisture in the air, the butterflies in your stomach when you do not quite know what to expect, the homesickness, and all the emotions that come with finding your way in a foreign culture—this is where students begin to have an authentic experience and create authentic relationships with each other as well as their teachers and informal educators. These are the moments that prepare students for the jobs of the future. One thing we do know about those jobs is that interaction with other people will not be going away anytime soon.

In addition to more money per pupil, we need to invest in providing each pupil with several of these authentic experiences per year. We need to drastically change where the money gets spent. According to educationdata.org, between 2017 and 2019 the US Department of Education's budget for "other education programs," which include vocational training and adult learning, dropped from $97.7 billion to $7.2 billion. It is precisely in this section of the budget where the exact opposite is required. This is where we must be willing to increase the amount of money per pupil and reevaluate where this money is being spent. Providing this type of experiential programming for students—so that they can engage with their intellectual, emotional, and spiritual responses, strengthening their connection to learning—is crucial to preparing them for future jobs.

Piaget

Jean Piaget was a Swiss educational philosopher known to most educators for his theory of cognitive development relative to children. Piaget's work included four stages of cognitive development. The age ranges are newborn to two years, two to six years, seven to eleven years, and twelve to fifteen years. Because Piaget's four stages of cognitive development end at fifteen years of age, we must rely upon Kolb's interpretation of Piaget, reviewing secondary education, student perceptions, benefits of experiential learning, and dual-knowledge theory (to be defined later in the book). The value of Piaget in this book is that all of the students I deal with have theoretically gone through the four stages of cognitive development, and their development has been shaped by their experiences, or not, depending on the group. Kolb summarizes Piaget nicely when he writes,

> The process of cognitive growth from concrete to abstract and from active to reflective is based on this continual transaction between assimilation and accommodation, occurring in successive stages, each of which incorporates what has gone before into a new, higher level of cognitive functioning (Kolb 1984, 23).

The cognitive development that Kolb and Piaget wrote about is essential to understanding experiential learning theory. It is the reflection Kolb mentions above that is of importance to this analysis and completes the cognitive development as it relates to the individual experience.

What role does discovery and exploration play in the student's experience?

Discovery is the process of finding something new, to be the first human to see, find, or simply be somewhere no other human has been before. Now this can also be a much more personal process. It can be an internal struggle to find purpose in a universe that does its best to hide your purpose from you. This is the essence of experience. This is how you determine what actually lights your soul on fire.

Each of the four stages builds on the advances and developments made in the previous stage. The advancement into the next stage of cognitive development is not necessarily interpreted based on age; rather, it is based on the experiences undertaken within the assigned time period. Kolb suggests that ". . . experiential learning is based on dual-knowledge theory: the empiricists' concrete experience, grasping reality by the process of direct apprehension, and the rationalists' abstract conceptualization, grasping reality via the mediating process of abstract conceptualization" (Kolb 1984, 101).

The debate between rationalist and empiricist philosophy conjures the great names of philosophic thought; on the rationalist side is Descartes and Spinoza, though Spinoza did argue against Descartes' mind-body dualism system, and on the empiricist side is Locke and Hobbes. Descartes, ever the rationalist, believed knowledge is gained through intuition and deductive reasoning. John Locke and other empiricists believed that all knowledge was discovered through empirical observation and experience.

Both are correct.

There isn't one correct method by which people acquire knowledge. It is logical to assume that knowledge can be achieved via the transit of many varied and diverse pathways. Piaget's theories exist at the crossroads of rationalist interpretation of experiential learning and empiricist interpretation of experiential learning; though, according to Kolb, ". . . Piaget's interactionism is decidedly rationalist in spirit" (Kolb 1984, 101).

So why does this debate, soundly grounded in philosophic tranquility, matter? How does it apply to our problem? The debate is important because recognition of what drives your passions can be determined using either method or some combination of methods derived from the post-experience reflection.

Experiential Reflection #2

The following is a day-by-day account of an experience offered by my current institution that I was lucky enough to be chosen to help lead. This differs from the experience in Turkey in that this is primarily led and sponsored by our institution rather than a third party. This experience includes two teachers and approximately a dozen or so students as well as our in-country fixers, guides, and drivers.

Day 1, Kuching, Sarawak, East Malaysia, Borneo

Kuching was my first glimpse of Southeast Asia. Before going, I felt a sense of timid nervousness mixed with full-on excitement. Kuching means "cat," according to Lemon (that's our guide). I wish I could remember what tribe he's from, but I can't. I liked Lemon. He was funny. We stay at the Lime Tree Hotel, nicer than I thought it would be. Come to think of it, the city was far more modern than I thought as well. It had Wi-Fi for Christ sake. (You see here my own preconceived biases and prejudices showing. If I had never been to Southeast Asia, if I had never had that experience, I may well think the same way today.) I was happy I was able to contact my wife and keep her abreast of my travels in Borneo. But having Wi-Fi also meant my students were not disconnected (and their teachers, if I'm being honest) from their tiny screens; I wanted them to connect to the culture, undistracted. On a side note, our program has since instituted a no technology policy on all programs, both foreign and domestic. The educational advantage for the students in highly apparent. Once the devices are gone, once they are disconnected, they instantly revert back to interacting regularly with their compatriots. They begin to play card games and others things. If they still had tech devices, this would never happen. Their heads go from staring down into a tiny screen to lifting up to experience the world around them.

Lemon and our driver, Slee (a Muslim man of faith), dropped us at the hotel. We checked in then met up to explore a little of the city and exchange some money—three ringgits equaled one dollar. As we walked through the city, it became all too clear we are in Southeast Asia. The city was dirty and developing. In the window of a store front, proudly displayed, was "SHARKS FIN." (Over the years, I have travelled to Southeast Asia twice for approximately twenty days each time, and I have struggled to find conservation efforts in the regions I've travelled. The Malaysian people have seemingly allowed endless intrusions by Chinese companies to destroy the land and water, poisoning the indigenous tribes upriver.) It is important for the students to see this, to feel what this is like. We lived among the indigenous tribes upriver which allowed for the students the experience first-hand what this feels like for those people.

One day, I was going to eat lunch with the boys on the trip. A man was frying fresh chicken in a wok, and we ventured inside. It was a great meal and wonderful introduction to Malaysian food. This is seemingly a mundane event, but the importance of eating the same food as the local populations is such and important aspect of learning and understanding any culture. We went back to the hotel and slept for a couple hours. We reconvened at 6 p.m. for dinner. We ate at an open-air seafood market called Top Shop. I had red snapper in a black pepper sauce with fried soft-shell crabs. The twelve-hour time difference was catching up to us. We . . . needed . . . sleep.

Day 2, Kuching, Sarawak, East Malaysia, Borneo

On our second day in Kuching, we visited an orangutan rehabilitation and conservation center. It was a short hike on paved roads from the parking lot into the area where we entered the jungle for the first time. We saw many orangutans. Orang means "man-of" and tan "forest." Orangutan actually means "man of the forest." We stayed there for an hour or so observing the amazing animals in their natural habitat and then headed back to the coach bus.

I remember thinking that I originally thought our encounters with the burnt-orange beasts of the jungle would be much closer up. I had misinterpreted what the experience would be like. I assumed the students would be working closely with scientists and conservationists around the animals. This highlights an issue with experiential education in general; when working with third party vendors in developing countries, you really never know what you're going to get until you get there.

Orangutans, we learned, share 96.4 percent of the same DNA sequence with human beings, homo sapiens. The second part of the day was far more interesting. We spent the remains of the day at a school. It was called Tunku Putra International School in Kuching. The students there were infinitely more focused on academics than our students. It was a window into the larger problem we see with American education. The larger problem of entitlement.

These students have classes in athletics, art, and music as well as academics, just as American students do. They are not only taking academic lessons. We could learn a lot from the Asian model. Some of our students are unmotivated and lazy and extremely selfish. I remember being embarrassed by some of their comments, questions, and answers during our visit. This is also a real example of real students experiencing the world and having an authentic interaction with their peers in another culture. While perhaps a bit embarrassing, it was indeed authentic. I also recall thinking I'd like to work with students like the ones at Tunku Putra International School. (These previous thoughts represent my initial thoughts upon experiencing this school in 2013. There is indeed much to admire in the Asian model of education, though experiential learning should be implemented into the system there as well.)

Day 3, Kuching, Sarawak, East Malaysia, Borneo/Iban Longhouse (joined by Paul and Uncle Denis)

We left Kuching and headed for the jungle. It was a four-and-a-half-hour ride in the coach to the jetty to take us to the first longhouse, and we made several stops along the way. The first stop was in a city called Serian. There, we found a wonderful example of a Southeast Asian outdoor open-air market consisting of seafood, poultry, fruits, and vegetables, all local and all fresh.

This represented my first true Asian market experience and I loved it. I loved it for the smells and the sounds and activity. It seemed alive with freshness. I bought some fried plantains that were excellent, though I craved to try something more exotic. I wasn't able to muster the courage. Perhaps that was a good instinct, considering some of the various gastrointestinal issues some experienced over the course of the expedition. Although, it is to be expected in such a foreign environment. Anytime you drastically change your routine and add unfamiliar food to your diet, these gastrointestinal issues will arise. Experiential learning trips are no different; it's all part of the experience.

Imagine the stares thirteen white kids, one African American kid, and one Asian American get in a Southeast Asian open-air market in the interior of Borneo. I gathered this was not a very common experience for the locals. The thought that jumps out here is that of the "other." It was, for our thirteen white students, most likely the first time they had been the minority and had felt the stares and felt the stigmatism that comes from being the "other" for once and experiencing that feeling of discomfort. We have to allow our students to be more confortable being uncomfortable.

The other expedition leader and I commented that if the kids weren't there, we could actually have some fun. We could have had a nice meal of street food at the market.

We stopped at a pepper farm, and more and more, I regret not buying some fresh pepper while I was there. It was a sprawling estate with vast green rolling hills. Hidden among the hills was the aging infrastructure required for processing the raw peppercorns into the fine granular substance we all have on all our tables.

Eventually, we arrived at the jetty and got our first glimpse of the Iban boatmen. The new river system was created through a hydroelectric dam, located directly behind the jetty. The creation of these dams has greatly impacted the Iban people's way of life. The Iban tribe are the notorious headhunters of Borneo, famous of course for taking head trophies of their enemies in war. Women and children were often the most prized heads because they were the most protected. This meant that the warrior battled and killed his way through countless enemies to reach the inner sanctum where the women and children were meant to be kept safe. (There will be more on this later.)

Our boat broke. The Iban boatman and his wife sitting in the bow of the boat paddled to the edge of the river so he could replace something called the "safety pin." I never did figure out what that meant. This happened many times while we were on the river and seemed to be a regular occurrence, so much so that the other boatmen would just leave their stranded comrade as though this was par for the course. I noticed that, when this happens, each of the men has a job. No one, other than the chief or headman, orders anyone around. They all simply know that each of their tasks or jobs will get done. The students on the trip are experiencing this as well and they don't fail to notice the efficiency of it all.

When we reached the jetty at the other end of our boat ride, our point of disembarkation, roughly forty-five minutes had passed. What followed was a simple twenty-minute hike along a wooden and concrete walkway until we reached the longhouse community. My first impression was negative; I admit that freely, and I own that initial reaction. It was far more modernized than I had ever expected it to be. They had windows, glass doors with knobs, electricity, and plumbing. They wore western clothes: Adidas, Nike, and various other Western brands. This brings me to a short commentary on the negative impacts of globalization on indigenous peoples. Not just in Borneo but all over the planet indigenous cultures are being lost to global brands like Adidas, McDonalds, and Starbucks. Entire cultures and languages and ways of life are being lost in the name of socioeconomic "progress." This is a regression of humanity.

This was my initial reaction. Writing now, years later, and years wiser, I have a somewhat different outlook. I offer the following question: who am I to wish these people back into abject poverty? My Westernized romantic vision of these people harkens to a period of imperialist oppression and total poverty. These modernities that I originally perceived as so offensive to my Western imperial perception are simple advances that add comfort to these people's lives.

I loved the longhouse culture and system of family. It is the closest-knit community I have seen. However, people do leave. The men, on Peselai, a coming of age journey. A journey, often months or years long when young men go off to prove themselves brave and worthy. This is a tradition mostly connected with the Dayak branch of the Iban people. For some perspective, I asked the young men among our students if they were ready for their journey. Does the American university system of education provide the same experience? Clearly not, nor is that its intended purpose, but the question set them thinking about entitlement and the advantages afforded to them through the simple accident of the location of their birth.

I really loved the Iban people. They are among the most welcoming cultures in the world. Their hospitality is legendary. Anyone can visit a longhouse and is welcome to stay as long as they wish. Anthropologists do this often.

The Iban are also among the most studied indigenous cultures on the planet. We met the headman when we arrived. I didn't ever catch his actual name, but we all called him Chief-Chief. He remained with for days and promptly invited us to have tea. It was Lipton. He also invited us to have rice wine. It was not the rocket fuel flavor that I had anticipated; rather, it was quite smooth and tasteful. It is in their culture to offer everything they have to their guests. It can present as badgering behavior at times (my Western individualized political linearity of thought showing through). But this is their custom. Each time they drink, they offer it to the entire room. They would be remiss if they didn't offer. This was explained to me by a man at the open-fire pit while he slowly roasted beef and chicken. We slept in the rooms of the longhouse with the families, side by side.

Day 4, Iban Longhouse Jungle Camp

In the morning, we had a simple breakfast. What we had escapes my memory. After this apparently unmemorable breakfast, we had a blowpipe demonstration; each of us attempted (but none of us were any good). I think I hit the small makeshift cardboard target one out of three times at a distance of ten to fifteen yards. These men can hit a target with enough power to kill whatever it is at 150 yards. An extremely impressive feat.

After this, we watched a demonstration of a good old-fashioned cockfight. I got it on video. This is important to the Iban not only for gambling purposes but also because each color rooster is known for different parts of the community. It was just a demonstration, and no animals were hurt in the filming. After this, we packed up our gear and headed back to the jetty. We hopped back in the longboats and began the trip to the point; there, we would begin our jungle trek. We had a lunch of fried chicken and rice, probably one of the little birds running around the longhouse, which means one less rooster wake-up call at 4 a.m. It was hot. So hot that I think my sweat was sweating.

We started our trek. It was meant to take roughly three and a half hours. In reality, it took us nearly six hours to complete the trek. Our slow progress was due to several factors.

First, we were mostly white Westerners and had no clue how to travel effectively or efficiently in the jungle.

Second, one of our kids got sick about thirty minutes into the trek. We had to nurse him for the next five and a half hours. I suspect it was a combination of heat exhaustion and dehydration. It is important for anyone who wishes to undertake the responsibility of taking students into the unknown that medical situations will occur. As a program leader it is your responsibility in the moment to care for the student as you have been trained and once in a relatively safe and stable environment, evaluate whether evacuation to more advanced medical services is required.

Third, we were a large group; in fact, we were the largest group that had ever done this particular Borneo trek.

The Iban headman, whom we called Chief Chief, Lemon, and Paul (another of our guides) moved through the jungle with ease. They had none of the technical hiking gear that we had and the Chief smoked clove cigarettes one after another the entire way. He wore

Adidas slip sandals and dressed entirely in cotton, and he kicked our ass up and down the trail. While smoking the entire time, the Chief also carried the sick kid's pack and all his gear. A man of action and of few words and even less fingers, he carried on for hours with this ridiculous feat. He was missing most of his right index finger. Eventually, after translation through Lemon, I learned it was lost in a chainsaw incident. He didn't turn off the chainsaw before attempting to fix a stuck chain.

Once we arrived at the camp, it was underwhelming at first. That is until one began to examine the camp with a more detailed eye. It was truly magnificent. The Iban had literally carved out a beautiful site in the jungle near a great swimming hole. They had lashed all our cots together in a row, all off the ground and each with its own mosquito netting. The bugs were not terrible; I've had worse experiences with mosquitoes in Panama City, Panama. We only had a few run-ins with the leaches, and as long as we had bug repellent on, we felt relatively protected. Of course, we all had bites at some point in the jungle, some from mosquitoes and some from unseen and unheard insects in the night.

They had a kitchen set up as well, and soon after we arrived, completely soaked to the bone with sweat, meat went on the grill. The grill was more of a lean-to sort of smoker. After the meat and fish had smoked for a while, it was covered with a green leaf for which I do not remember the name of the plant. We ate Iban BBQ, had some rice wine, and went to bed early.

On a side note, earlier in the evening, Chief, Lemon, Paul, and Luweng from the next longhouse (the one we were supposed to trek to the following day) called the co-leader and me over to their camp. The Chief, of course, had a plastic water bottle filled with rice wine. He had cut the top off his bottle with his pareng and fashioned a makeshift shot glass out of it. I was obliged to partake in multiple glasses of this rice wine. He had also prepared some smoked fish. He handed me one and then took the head off and ate it. I ate the rest of the fish. For the next one, I took the head off it and ate it, and he ate the body. We all had a laugh and ate the rest of the smoked fish.

Day 5, Iban Jungle Camp, Borneo Adventure Lodge, and Longhouse II

Instead of the six-hour trek from the jungle camp to Borneo Adventure Lodge (BAL) and longhouse II, we negotiated via our guides with Chief to use the longboats to take us there. We had a sick kid and there was no way he could have made the trek. We had to use the boats; we couldn't get halfway into a six-hour trek through the Borneo jungle and have this kid pass out. It was the only logical option, though it wasn't a foregone conclusion. We still had to navigate some fairly treacherous cultural boundaries. The Iban don't do it like everyone else. The Chief spoke only to our guides; then they spoke to us. After all was settled (we would use the boats), we all stood and shook hands. All of our words were good enough.

That morning, we broke camp, and by that, I mean the Iban broke camp. We walked a bit through the river until it was deep enough to float the longboats and jumped in for a two-and-a-half hour ride. We stopped on several occasions to be sure all the boats stayed together; then we finally arrived at the Borneo Adventure Lodge. It was a nice place with amenities. Showers, bathrooms, mattresses, mosquito nets, a kitchen, coffee, and tea available most hours of the day.

We had a lazy day around the lodge. The boys ended up playing in the river with the children from the longhouse just across the river. The two establishments were connected via a bridge spanning the river. But that physical connection seemed artificial, built to connect two disparate worlds—the well-to-do Western tourists lounging around in relative luxury at the Borneo Adventure Lodge, while just across the river were those living in abject poverty. One in the twenty-first century; the other, not.

Clearly there had been some kind of business arrangement between the interested parties. The longhouse had satellite TV; the BAL did not. The BAL had showers and toilets; the longhouse did not. Go figure. Again, part of me finds the intrusion of the twenty-first century in this indigenous culture to be nauseating and sad, but on the other hand, how dare I wish these people back into discomfort and abject poverty. Which of these sentiments is worse? I do not know.

That evening, we went over to the longhouse, much bigger than the first, and met the headman. He was very old and probably didn't actually run the day-to-day activities of the longhouse anymore. The Iban have a wonderful sense of *let well enough alone*. This longhouse consisted of maybe twenty-five to thirty-five families, some living in separate houses outside the longhouse.

Day 6, Borneo Adventure Lodge, Longhouse II, and Longhouse III

We loaded up in the longboats after a forgettable breakfast. We've had chicken and rice at least once every single day. This is a great revelation for our students, who are accustomed to a much greater variety of food choices in a single day. Most of the world, once you get beyond the Western developed countries, subsists on some combination of chicken and rice each and every day, sometimes a different combination of the same meal for each meal.

We took the longboats to longhouse III. This was the most interesting longhouse that we visited. We met with the headman, and he agreed to show us the skulls collected by his grandfather, a great Iban warrior and headhunter. He showed us the skulls. There was an eerie feeling in the room. One of them still had the hair on it. If you're like me, you just Googled how long it takes hair to decompose. The answer is sometimes as long as two years. That's not the answer I was looking for. Does that mean this gentleman had been dead perhaps only two years? Probably not. We hope not. Well . . .

We held a spear. A spear that had taken lives. This man had a long, thinning, gray beard that reached down past his chest, nearly all the way to his navel. He was balding, with long gray hair, shirtless, and wearing green Adidas shorts. I enjoyed meeting this man immensely. He was old and had to climb into an overhead storage space to retrieve the skulls. He climbed like a spider. The agility and deftness with which the Iban people move is astonishing, certainly a trait evolved over millennia, adapting to life in the jungles of Borneo. It's seemingly embedded in their DNA—balance, agility, quickness, strength, all superior within their environment.

After this visit, we headed back to the longboats, all of us quiet and reflecting on what we had just seen—a glimpse into a different moment in time and a vastly different cultural history. We swam and had lunch at a beautiful waterfall. In the pool created by the waterfall, there were little fish that would swim up and nibble on your skin. If you stood still, it was possible to collect ten or twelve of them on your legs and feet, a more natural exfoliate you will not find elsewhere. It tickled more than anything else.

Lunch was chicken, sticky rice in bamboo shoots, and fruit. After lunch, we piled back into the longboats and the boatmen poled our way back downriver through the small rapids. The river knowledge of these men is immense. They know every nook and cranny of the waterways. These waterways essentially serve as their highway system within the depths of the Borneo jungle. To you or me, the river would seem impassable; this is not the case for the Iban boatmen's trained eye.

We stopped downriver and disembarked from the longboats just as a torrential downpour unloaded from the darkening and menacing skies above. We all pulled out rain gear. As it turns out, there's a reason the Iban do not wear rain gear, and it's not because they can't get it. It's because it doesn't matter. Everything on our bodies and in our backpacks was completely waterlogged within minutes.

The trek started with a steep technical ascent. It was long and the rain made it harder. The Borneo jungle soil is sort of a red clay. It's slippery enough when it's dry but add water, and you've got a terribly difficult trek. The kids did well—no complaints. It was a jungle hike I'll never forget, in weather that can only be described as raining cats and dogs. We arrived safely, soaked to the bone, though I had taken a fall roughly twenty minutes from the lodge.

We played spades. The co-leader and I taught them a lesson; they were inexperienced, and we beat them badly. We went back to longhouse II that night to bare witness to a traditional Iban ceremony and dance. It was the dance that represents the return home of the warriors and hunters. The women and some men play instruments while a male warrior (also a hunter) plays out his most recent escapades in a traditional style dance wearing traditional Iban garb. A female will then do the same. I have stills and a video of this event. I can't help but feel as though the entire thing was staged for our benefit. In fact, I know that it was. I'm pretty sure the first guy was at least mildly intoxicated. It's sad. Their culture has been reduced to putting on little shows for Western tourists.

I ended up purchasing a few authentic souvenirs that the Iban would often offer us. Lemon thanked us profusely for contributing to their little economy. It's not actually authentic. It does offer a microcosm into the history of their people and culture, and perhaps some good may come from the fact that it connects the youngest members of their families with their cultural past.

The "Longhair"

One of the men at longhouse II intrigued me. He was a younger man, maybe upper thirties or low forties. He had long straight black hair, a plethora of tattoos, and was in excellent physical shape. He worked in the bow of the boats and was masterful with the long pole. He seemed to command a bit of respect from the other Iban men, though he was not the headman. The headman these days, as much as anything else, has to be a politician. This intense longhaired fellow did not appear to have the slightest inclination or disposition for political dealings of the modern ilk. He seemed . . . stuck in time, a throwback to the past, a modern-day incarnation of old Iban ways of life, born in the wrong century.

Day 7, Borneo Adventure Lodge, Longhouse II/, Jetty, and Kuching

We left our friends at the longhouses and said goodbye to our Iban brethren. It should be noted that Chief Half Finger left the previous day with a compatriot in a drunken stupor. Lemon pointed out that their wives would be quite upset. Some things are universal. We hopped into the longboats one more time and headed downriver to the jetty near the hydroelectric dam where we first met our Iban hosts. Again, I am reminded of the negative impacts of globalization on the indigenous people of Borneo. It's not just Borneo; these activities are occurring all over the world. Dam projects and logging activities are increasingly prevalent in the less-industrialized world. It's economic imperialism. Same exploitative concepts of imperialism—different methods. In Borneo, it's the Chinese, but the Malay are just as much to blame for seemingly selling their country to the highest bidder. The Chinese are chewing up natural resources and leaving behind a once-pristine and now shattered environment on one of the most biodiverse islands in the world. It saddens me that if I go back to that place, it will almost certainly be worse off than when I first visited. What of this beautiful culture will be left? Nothing but staged displays for the tourists.

Day 8, Travel Day, Kuching, Kota Kinabalu, and Tawau

We flew from Kuching through Kota Kinabalu to Tawau. From the little bit of Tawau we saw, it seemed to be littered with slums. We did not leave the hotel. We had dinner at a decent hotel buffet called the Promenade and turned in early.

Day 9, Tawau and Pom Pom Island

We took a bus to the jetty, this time on the sea, not a river, in the seaside town of Samporna. It seemed to be a nice enough town. We got into a boat called the *Lady Zaidah* and within a short thirty- or forty-five-minute boat ride, we arrived at Pom Pom Island. Idyllic is perhaps the best word to describe this place. I imagine it's typical of many islands in the South Pacific. Is this considered the South Pacific? Perhaps not. Anyway, I have no way of knowing if Pom Pom is typical as I've never been to the South Pacific.

When we arrived, we checked in and the dive masters checked our dive certification cards. We changed and got geared up for our check dive. This was a dive to be sure we were weighted correctly and to get comfortable in the water with new gear. We learned the hand signals they preferred to use, which were a bit different than what I was trained to use, but it wasn't a problem.

The three dive masters our group worked with were Graham from South Africa, Matt from France, and Zainal from Malaysia. My group included three students, with Zainal as our dive master. He was by far the coolest, though still professional, of the three, and I was happy to have him lead our dives over the next few days. Once the check dive was over, we all settled into our rooms and had a nice lunch. We had our second dive of the day at 3:00 p.m. It was truly a fucking mosaic of life. Dive two was fifty-two minutes long. Pom Pom was your classic beach dive spot. We stayed at Celebes Beach Resort, which shared the small island with Pom Pom Resort, a far posher resort than where we stayed. Good. One of the primary goals of experiential learning is to create an experience that offers students a chance to get outside their comfort zone, to get comfortable being uncomfortable. There are three zones I like to tell my students about. The comfort zone, the growth zone and the danger zone. The comfort zone is where dreams go to die. The growth zone is where the authentic learning takes place and the danger zone is where our fight or flight instincts take over and we are incapable of rational thought and therefore are incapable of learning. As program leaders, it is vitally important to create experiences that are in the growth zone and nearing the edge of the danger zone. That's where the authentic relationships are built and where the authentic learning occurs.

Day 10, Pom Pom Island

We settled into Pom Pom Island routine. We'd wake up around 7 or 7:30 a.m. and have breakfast. Then we would jump on the dive boats with our crew and do two morning dives. On the second dive that day, we saw a massive barracuda, the highlight of my dive experience. We got extremely close, and I got great photos and video. We also saw several green sea turtles and hawksbill turtles. They are amazing creatures of the sea, and we certainly should do everything we can to conserve these animals. We also did an afternoon dive, and this would become our routine for the next day or so. Fletcher, from Tropical Research and Conservation Centre, came over that night to give us a talk on the ongoing turtle conservation efforts. I retired to my room after the talk.

TRACC

TRACC was a conservation group based on the island. They had two main goals:

First, track the turtles that nest on the island.

Second, devise creative methods for regrowing coral around the island.

Unfortunately, most of the coral around the island had been badly damaged. It was literally blown up by local fishermen in an effort to catch fish more effectively. An efficient yet terribly destructive method. This had been a theme of our trip to Malaysia. The group itself seemed a bit dubious at best. There didn't seem to be any actual scientists there. There were about five staff members, and the rest were volunteers that stayed roughly a month at a time.

As we were leaving, a group of Chinese volunteers showed up. The staff were not very excited. It seems it had not gone well the last time a group of Chinese volunteers arrived. Elaboration was not forthcoming. The organization seemed to be led by a guy called Johnny. He was a replacement of some kind, a person who knew the daughter of a guy called Steve, who appeared to be the person who underwrote this whole operation. Like I said, dubious.

Day 11, Pom Pom Island

We fell into a routine—breakfast, two morning dives, lunch, and an afternoon dive. Between dives the previous day, we had walked over to the TRACC headquarters—and I use that term loosely—to help build some artificial reefs. The process was interesting. They were trying all kinds of creative methods for reef building. They had bags of dry concrete mix. We simply added sand and water to the mix and poured the mixture into the molds. While the concrete was still wet, we sticked bottles or sticks into the concrete and let the mixture dry. The mixture was not ready or dry enough to be placed on the bottom that day. It would have to wait.

We completed our final dive on Pom Pom Island's northern tip. We dove here in order to survey the area where our artificial reefs would be placed and to see previous examples of what our work would become. That was our final night on the island.

Dinner consisted of barbecue fish, chicken, and beef, smoked over a grill of open-wood coals. A fine meal.

Zainal

Zainal was a great dive master for our group. He was attentive and patient when we asked questions. He was, perhaps more importantly, attentive under water. He checked our air repetitively while making sure we also had some responsibility for checking our own gauges at regular intervals. He was fond of the phrase "Don't be shy; take your time but be quick about it." He would often follow it with a wry smile and his distinctive laugh.

Zainal is Malaysian. It seemed that he was at odds with Graham (who fancied himself the boss) more than once. Zainal was far more detail oriented underwater, pointing out the smallest creatures instead of crusing by like the others. He made me feel at ease, which is important underwater. I tried to emulate him beneath the surface in an effort to make the most out of the air I had. I tried to focus on being confident and loose rather than anxious and tight. It didn't always work, but it made me feel good to try. I liked Zainal; I won't soon forget him.

As we parted ways, I told him to be good and have fun. It makes me sad that I will more than likely never see him again.

Day 12, Pom Pom Island and Kota Kinabalu

In the morning, we went out on the dive boat to watch the TRACC guys dive and put the artificial reefs we made on the seafloor. Zainal actually did something incredibly stupid tying the big boat to the TRACC little boat and pulling the anchor free, almost completely screwing up the operation. The two girls in our group, the co-leader, and I swam over to the little TRACC boat to help lower the blocks of concrete to the bottom. The girls and the co-leader went back to the dive boat while I stayed on the TRACC boat to help the British girl get the motor started; then I swam back over to the dive boat. This little experience was incredibly valuable, though it may not seem so. There are any number of lessons in that small experience. The value of the big-picture experience can sometimes, if not always, be found in adding up the significance of the small moments like the one previously detailed.

We had lunch and caught the 1:30 p.m. boat back to Semporna. We loaded the bags in buses and headed for the Tawau airport. We were off to Kota Kinabalu for two nights. We arrived in Kota Kinabalu late due to weird flight delays leaving Tawau.

Tawau Departure Lounge

It felt like a classic movie scene. I felt a bit like an expat sitting in a classic Southeast Asian departure lounge from some romantic 1940s

World War II classic starring Bogart and Bacall. I was drinking a four-ringgit cappuccino in an open-air airport lounge, reflecting on our journey. The only thing missing was the cigarette and fedora.

Day 13, Kota Kinabalu

We spent the day in KK. It was a much more cosmopolitan than Kuching. After sleeping in and having breakfast around 9:30 a.m., we went off to change some money and do some shopping in the mall across from our hotel and the central market. The central market wasn't blowing anybody's skirt up, so we left there a bit disappointed, hoping that the night market would provide something more. It did. The night market had everything. The textiles (Batik) were amazing works of art as well as some of the other goods on display in the market. The best part of the night market was the fish. Every type of seafood you could possibly want or even imagine was there. We saw a massive tuna being chopped for steaks; we all wanted sashimi, but we realized bad fish the day before two full days of travel would have been a risk.

I enjoyed the fish market immensely. It was interesting listening to the stall owners calling out the prices for each type of fish on display. It was reminiscent of the market we visited in Serian but way better. The sights and smells and sounds created a slight sensory overload. The city, at that moment in time, had come alive, just as the sun was setting over the inlet. It was a tranquil feeling.

I watched a little girl, no more than seven or eight, use a small filet knife to clean two small fish. Her younger brother came over and handed her another fish. Imagine this scene in the United States in the twenty-first century. Someone would have called Child Protective Services. We've gotten soft and too comfortable in our relative wealth. We need to be more comfortable being uncomfortable. It wasn't so long ago in our country when similar scenes played out and were looked upon with the same impartial indifference as this scene in Southeast Asia. What has been the impact on our own culture of having reared so many generations in too much comfort? Entitlement and generations of people obsessed with maintaining or improving their comfort level rather than exploring beyond their comfort zone inhibits growth and the discovery of what truly sets their souls on fire.

Day 14, Kota Kinabalu and Singapore

We left Borneo. I had mixed feelings; I was truly ready to go home but not yet ready to leave Southeast Asia. The people I met along the way had been the salt of the earth. I was already ready to plan another trip.

We had a ten-hour layover in Singapore. We decided to pass through customs just to get our passport stamped. We cleared customs and all looked at each other. We were all fairly seasoned travelers. The stamp in our passports would be a constant reminder that we faked it. We jumped on a train into the city center. We couldn't help it; we sort of had to. We wandered around for a bit, inadvertently found Chinatown. It was like most Chinatowns. We cruised through in an hour or so and stopped to look through a few shops; then we headed back to the airport. It was definitiely an experience worth having, and I can look at myself in the mirror and know that I hadn't faked Singapore. Forty-eight hours, later I was home.

The experiences described above should be embedded in the curriculum of every student, even our youngest learners, albeit age-appropriate, according to Piaget's models. These are the experiences that create the authenticity required to determine and develop a student's passions.

Lewin

Kurt Lewin was an educational theorist who wrote widely on experiential learning theory. He is among the philosophical giants of experiential learning espoused by David Kolb. His model is quite similar to that of Dewey, though Dewey goes a bit deeper into the developmental process than does Lewin. As noted by Kolb, there are two main points worth mentioning in Lewin's experiential learning model:

> First is its emphasis on *here-and-now concrete experience* to validate and test abstract concepts. Immediate personal experience is the focal point for learning, giving life, texture, and subjective personal meaning to abstract concepts and at the same time providing a concrete, publicly shared reference point for testing the implications and validity of ideas created during the learning process. When human beings share an experience, they can share it fully, concretely, *and* abstractly (Kolb 1984, 21).

Lewin's model of experiential learning is the closest to what secondary educators try to provide for their students. Dewey, Piaget, and Lewin are intricately connected, and all offer influential philosophical foundations.

First is Piaget's penchant for reflective analysis of the experience. Reflection is absolutely a key component of gaining the most out of the experience. Not a climb goes by that Alex Honnold does not eventually write about. It requires a discipline that has been lost in the cacophony of distraction conveyed to us via the small super computers we all carry in our pockets.

Dewey and Lewin also wax poetic on various occasions regarding the importance of the reflective process and the overall learning landscape. Lewin refers to this process as the *feedback processes*. Kolb considers Lewin's feelings on reflection: "Lewin and his followers believed that much individual and organizational ineffectiveness could be traced ultimately to a lack of adequate feedback processes" (Kolb 1984, 22).

In other words, the cause of organizational ineffectiveness is as significant as lack of reflection. This can be applied school-wide to the organization itself as well as to the models of experiential education opportunities provided to the students.

Dewey, Piaget, and Lewin all believed that organization is key to the development of a viable experiential learning theory. All three men were multiplicitous in their convictions. Dewey, a mixture of traditional and progressive thought, leaned toward the progressive on most occasions; though, he was not a proponent of acting on an idea simply because the term progressive was placed in front of the concept (i.e., progressive education).

Dewey was a lifelong pragmatist. Piaget was a mixture of rationalist and empiricist thought, often invoking Rene Descartes and his advocacy of abstract conceptualism in the later stages of development and John Locke and his concrete experiences in the initial stages of development.

Lewin brings it all together. His model is the unification of all three philosophical giants of experiential learning. The Lewinian model's focus on immediate concrete experience in order to explain, confirm, and ultimately test abstract concepts is the tie that binds experiential learning at the secondary level. Experiential learning at the secondary level includes a curricular component, the experiential opportunity, and proper reflection. The writings of John Dewey, Jean Piaget, and Kurt Lewin can be interpreted in such ways that they include all three ingredients for successful experiential learning at the secondary level.

The Role of Eastern Philosophy

As the years have worn on, and I think more about the next phases of my career and life, I seem to have arrived at a very Eastern place—not in the sense of physical geography but in the internalized philosophical sense.

One of the greatest moments that I experience while leading experiential education trips, and this happens all over the world, is my student's realization that time is not a linear concept outside of the Western world. This phenomenon is an incredible realization. I fell in love with the phraseology of the Italian writer Paolo Cognetti in his recent book *Without Ever Reaching the Summit*. He writes, "After a while, as happens in Nepal, the sensation of wasting time becomes one of adapting to a different flow of time." I have found this to be applicable in most of the non-Western world.

The Eastern philosophies, whether it be religious or some other aspect of the culture, are far more circular (as opposed to linear) in nature. Lines, by their nature, divide. Principally, that is their purpose. Take borders, for instance; on one side of the imaginary international political construct is one nation-state, and on the other side, another nation-state. This line divides, as does the line of time. It divides old and young, it divides fast and slow, and it divides one from another. This linear relationship with time is a Western political construct. The creation of the nation-state and these, sometimes, arbitrary lines and divisions on a map are also Western political constructs. The circular nature of Eastern philosophies such as Taoism and Buddhism offer a distinct cultural relationship with time. First, circles are inclusive and not divisive. They are, by their nature, enclosed. This seems to cut off what is outside the circle. But that is not what's happening. The pervasive linear thinking in Western thought is divisive. It has had the unfortunate impact of dividing man and nature, for example. In Eastern circular thought, the two perceived opposites, man and nature, are enclosed and thereby merged as one within the circle. This is the yin and the yang.

Where do these ways of thought originate? Western linear thinking originates with the great thinkers of ancient times including, but not limited to, Aristotle and Plato. Kenneth Liberman presents the concept of egoism embedded in western political thought. The concept of the *I*, as in "I think" or "I believe," creates an egoism in our thought processes, and the origin of this can be found in Jacques Derrida's "coupling of Judaism and Hellenism." According to Derrida, the Jewish philosophies and traditions gave humanity the individual soul while it was the Greek democracy, such as it was, that gave humanity the individual citizen, the free thinker (Liberman 1989). This marriage resulted in the pervasiveness of the *I* in Western political thought. It is the Hellenistic and thereby Greek piece of this that is of interest here. Now, in order for this to work, there are several assumptions we must all accept. We must operate under the assumption that classical Athenian political thought greatly influenced Hellenistic political thought even as Hellenistic schools of philosophy began to develop new blueprints for philosophical thought.

According to Liberman, the Greek democracies are responsible for the introduction of some level of civil liberties to certain segments of the society. But there were limits; too much free inquiry can be a dangerous thing (Liberman 1989). Socrates, a man perhaps most well known as an independent and free thinker, was put to death for that very reason. Despite the unfortunate demise of Socrates, the *self* became the center of Western political thought. Citizens are most concerned with how they themselves will connect to the *other*, the barbarian. In classical and Hellenistic Greece, the *other* was the Persians. How the *other* is viewed is connected directly to individuals' perception based on their own experience. Perception, then, for the individual, is his or her own (self) reality.

Professor Zuo Biao of Shanghai Maritime University argues the Western political theories of dividing the world into two opposing parts. In contrast to the Western worldview, we find the writings of Lao Tzu. Lao Tzu, founder of Taoism, lived approximately 500 years prior to Christ and wrote a series of philosophical lessons that are still accessible today. The writings are referred to as the *Tao Te Ching*. This piece of work is the seminal instruction manual for living within a circular philosophy. Action and reflective thought are essential to understanding the *Tao Te Ching*, just as they are in experiential education. Think of the pre-experience preparation, the experience itself, and thoughtful reflection as the triumvirate or circular pattern of experiential education. Similarly, the *I Ching* is just as important in cyclical thought and leadership. The "sixty-four gua represent sixty-four different stages in a connected, rising and falling sequence of cyclic change." The main theme of this text is that all things are in a constant state of change. Everything is increasingly moving forward. Again, a rising and falling, opposite sides of the all-encompassing circle.

A line, in geometric terms, is straight, possesses no thickness, and continues infinitely in both directions. This ongoing, always-onward linearity is where Western and especially American individualism comes from. In American thought, the individual is the prime actor, and the individual makes decisions based on what's best for that individual. This is routinely seen as a positive in regard to the freedom of individuals to make their own choices. The negative impact rears its ugly head when individuals are asked to behave a certain way for the greater good. This is often perceived as a slight against the freedom of individual choice.

Do not individuals in a society owe it to that society, and the others living within it, to take action that improves and protects it against something that would destroy it? Are our civil liberties allowing for the destruction of the society that protects those very civil liberties? In Western and specifically the American interpretation of this way of thinking, achieving individual greatness outweighs most everything else.

The circular nature of the Eastern worldview embodied by the concept of the yin and yang of Taoism is not about individual greatness; rather, it is about community greatness being achieved together when one is focused inwardly—not outwardly. Linearity and individuality are outwardly focused while circularity and community are inwardly focused concepts.

These concepts are not limited to Taoism; there are many similar ideas and symbols to be found in Buddhism, as well as Confucianism. In the case of Buddhism, look no further than the prayer wheel. The purpose of the prayer wheels is to gather and perhaps reinvigorate good karmas and ultimately eliminate bad karmas on the path to ultimate spiritual wisdom. The circular nature of the prayer wheel itself shows the belief in the cyclical nature of karma, the importance of cleansing oneself of bad karmas and gathering good karmas. In Confucianism, we have the idea of *ritual*. These rituals seek to embed the idea that social constructs regulate the individual in much the same way governments seek, from time to time, to regulate business, all in an effort to reign in the linear individuality of the business owner and favor the common good of the workers. There is no way to separate oneness from noneness. The importance of this cyclical philosophic thought to experiential education is seen most clearly when applied to the triumvirate of pre-experience preparation, the experience itself, and the post-experience reflection.

Kolb

David A. Kolb's *Experiential Learning: Experience as the Source of Learning and Development* is largely a literary review of Dewey, Piaget, and Lewin; although, Kolb does add to Piaget's concepts of apprehension versus comprehension with regard to the acquisition of authentic knowledge through experience.

In other words, the appreciation of apprehended knowledge is much different than critical comprehension. Experiential learning can be the force that draws the two together in order to attain authentic knowledge of a particular subject matter. Kolb writes, "As we will see, knowledge and truth result not from the preeminence of one of these knowing modes over the other but from the intense coequal confrontation of both modes" (Kolb 1984, 105).

Bart P. Beaudin and Don Quick write in their paper "Experiential Learning: Theoretical Underpinnings," that "Kolb describes experiential learning as a four-part process, where the learner is asked to engage themselves in a new experience, actively reflect on that experience, conceptualize that experience and integrate it with past experiences" (Beaudin & Quick 1995, 11). Beaudin and Quick go on to suggest, "The facilitator's job is to guide them through each part in an ever-increasing level, expanding their learning of a topic" (Beaudin & Quick 1995, 12).

The educator is therefore engaged in the experiential learning opportunity with the student from start to finish, through all the processes of moderate curricularized instruction, through the experiential learning opportunity, and finally through the reflective period. We guide them through from the comfort zone to the growth zone and then to the edge of the danger zone.

Dewey also writes on acquisition of knowledge, thereby connecting himself with Kolb. Again, in Dewey's *Experience & Education*, he is advocating not for one model of education over another; rather, he is advocating for the organization of a theory of experiential learning that connects multiple modes of knowledge acquisition. Concerning acquisition of knowledge, he writes,

> As an individual passes from one situation to another, his world, his environment, expands or contracts. He does not find himself living in another world but in a different part or aspect of one and the same world. What he has learned in the way of knowledge and skill in one situation becomes an instrument of understanding and dealing effectively with the situations which follow. The process goes on as long as life and learning continue [and includes] knowledge of what has happened in similar situations in the past, a knowledge obtained partly by recollection and partly from the information, advice, and warning of those who have had a wider experience (Dewey 1938, 44–69).

Acquisition of authentic knowledge via experiential learning is accomplished through moderate curricular support of the experiential learning opportunity, the opportunity itself, and proper reflection—all of which are advocated by the philosophical giants of experiential learning.

There are those who disagree with Kolb. Reijo Miettinen, in his article "The Concept of Experiential Learning and John Dewey's Theory of Reflective Thought and Action," written in 2000 in the *International Journal of Lifelong Education*, offers a critique of Kolb's interpretation of Dewey, Piaget, and Lewin.

Miettinen regards the characteristics that define experiential learning:

"Without a doubt, the two concepts that characterize the approach most clearly are experience and reflection" (Miettinen 2000, 54). He believes in the basic constructs of the theory of experiential learning but disagrees with Kolb on his interpretation of the three philosophical giants of experiential learning, mostly with his interpretation of Dewey. Miettinen particularly takes issue with Kolb from an epistemological standpoint, with Kolb's interpretation of Dewey's model for the acquisition of authentic knowledge. Miettinen writes,

> In this paper, I shall evaluate the concept of experience, primarily from an epistemological point of view, that is, as a representation of learning and the process of gaining new knowledge. I will argue that in the light of the philosophical studies on the ways of gaining new knowledge of the world, the model of experiential learning is inadequate (Miettinen 2000, 54).

Kolb writes on learning and knowledge,

> Learning is the process whereby knowledge is created through the transformation of experience. This definition emphasizes several critical aspects of the learning process as viewed form the experiential perspective. First is the emphasis on the process of adaptation and learning as opposed to content or outcomes. Second is that knowledge is a transformation process, being continuously created and recreated, not an independent entity to be acquired or transmitted. Third, learning transforms experience in both its objective and subjective forms (Kolb 1938, 38).

According to Miettinen, Kolb's theories have suffered the most criticism from an epistemological standpoint. "This epistemological criticism and discussion concerning man's possibility of obtaining new knowledge about the world, is the most relevant issue for any theory of experience" (Miettinen 2000, 62). Miettinen is suggesting not only that Kolb has misinterpreted the meaning of Dewey assertions but also that the entirety of experiential learning theory is flawed, not taking into account the latest studies on scientific philosophy.

The literature regarding global travel among secondary education is scarce, if not barely existent. This is probably because secondary educators engaged in this experiential learning lack the time required for scholarly publication, as do most of the program directors in these institutions. There is, however, myriad literature on global travel as an opportunity for experiential learning for higher education. Most of it deals with the possible outcomes. In other words, it attempts to glean some measure of value from the global experience.

In the *Journal of Teaching in Travel & Tourism*, Stoner, Tarrant, Perry, Stoner, Wearing, and Lyons published a study titled "Global Citizenship as a Learning Outcome of Educational Travel" in 2013. The authors contend the goal and ultimate outcome of educational travel should be the creation of global citizenship. The purpose of the paper is to show universities that they need to adequately prepare their graduates with the skills necessary to compete for top careers in a more globalized society. To foster this global mindset, the universities developed the study abroad program. The authors argue ". . . that short term, experiential educational travel programs provide a critical platform to foster global citizenship when coupled with sound pedagogy" (Stoner & Tarrant et al. 2013, 149).

The interesting piece of this argument for me is the inclusion of pedagogy as a factor in the success of the program. The other interesting piece is the time frame, short term. As a secondary level educator, this is exciting because it lends credence to the programs I have led over the last fourteen years. These programs range from ten to fourteen days. Fourteen days is about the time a person starts to feel comfortable in a new culture and a new place while at the same time experiencing feelings of homesickness. Certain parts of life begin to become routine. This can take longer, of course, sometimes much longer. These short-term programs are sometimes criticized due to the lack of time required to truly engage in a culture. There are experiential education advocates and philosophers who believe in much longer programs lasting months. There is value for students in both formats. There is obviously a deeper connection to the culture the longer one is in country, but that does not mean the shorter programs are not valuable.

There is an argument that the hindrance to the global travel program at the secondary level is time—that there is not enough time for the educators to make the experience valuable to the students. Stoner *et al* suggest successful short-term programs are possible at the higher education level. If the goal of the program I am principally a part of is to prepare students for higher education and beyond, then surely the program is essentially preparing the students for short-term or long-term global travel learning programs such as study abroad at the higher education level.

Charles A. Salter and Allan I. Teger published a study in the journal *Sociometry* in 1975 titled "Change in Attitudes Toward Other Nations as a Function of the Type of International Contact." The authors set out to test a hypothesis by controlling for two problems with previous studies: "(a) the confusion between genuine and superficial contact, and (b) the failure to specify the dimensions of contact and attitudinal measurement" (Salter & Teger 1975, 213).

The authors believe that the results of previous studies are flawed because they didn't take into account the type of contact and because they failed to address the issue that some participants may have had negative experiences. The authors write, "Although it is reasonable to hypothesize that genuine contact leads to attitude enhancement, the positive or negative aspects (valence) of the contact experience are also important" (Salter & Teger 1975, 214). This is important because the authors are attempting to gauge participant perception, whether they had a positive or negative experience. The authors continue,

> . . . positive and negative experiences can cause corresponding attitude change towards objects having no direct connection with the experience, apparently through a generalization of

affect. Thus, under negative conditions, contact might be expected to result in negative attitude change, even if the contact is genuine (Salter & Teger 1975, 214).

This finding can strike fear into the discerning secondary-level educator involved in these global travel opportunities whose main purpose is to provide the students with the best possible experiential learning opportunity. Despite all best efforts to the contrary, the perceptions and prejudices of the student may indeed be too entrenched to overcome. The experience may strengthen these preconceptions instead of remove them.

The negative thoughts may remain, but it is doubtful that they learned nothing. It is important for the program leader to maintain the goals of the program, keeping in mind that the students may not show appreciation in the moment; that may not come until much later in life. Whether their cognitive development allows them to appreciate the experience in the moment or years later, mission accomplished.

Richard Holtzman, in his study titled "Experiential Learning in Washington, D.C.: A Study of Student Motivations and Expectations" published in the journal *Transformative Dialogues: Teaching & Learning Journal* in 2011, explains what motivates students to participate in experiential learning opportunities. He uses student participation in the 2009 presidential inauguration as his model. While this experience is not global, the five motivations Holtzman finds are useful. His five motivations are

1. A 'once-in-a-lifetime' opportunity.

2. Increase their knowledge and understanding of American politics.

3. Make them better citizens and/or more informed voters.

4. Aid their future careers.

5. Offer an experiential learning opportunity that could not be gained in the classroom (Holtzman 2011, 6–9).

I expect these motivations would be similar in the case of most experiential learning opportunities. The goal would simply be changed from a greater understanding of American culture and politics to a greater understanding of the culture of the destination.

Lucia Ames Mead, writing in the *Journal of Education* in 1928, espoused the value of travel. Her critiques of America and of the American abroad and their feelings toward the international system could be transplanted into an article in 2021, and the only clue to their antiquity would be the wide and lofty language of a bygone age. She writes,

> What can he do to promote international good will on a tour designed especially for recreation and general culture? It is, unhappily, quite possible to tour Europe and come home with minute knowledge about hotels and shops, operas and dinners, and with a head full of guidebook statistics, but with the mind empty of any new ideas or emotions which have enlarged one's culture, freed one from prejudice, or given one respect for anything not measured in dollars and cents (Mead 1928, 464–465).

Mead expounds the virtue of genuine contact. According to Mead,

> The real surprises will come as one converses in out-of-the-way places, and on the train, preferably in a third-class car, with plainly dressed folk, perhaps artists and scientists, about their everyday life and political and social outlook (Mead 1928, 465).

She contends that American citizens are at a massive disadvantage entering a more globalized world even in 1928. Mead suggests the moving picture shows on Sundays have made it impossible to surprise someone with new information. She writes this type of activity takes place ". . . in a world which generalizes quickly from small data" (Mead 1928, 465). Her sentiment predicts modern social media culture. How many times do people share articles on social media that they haven't read? Social media has created a culture in which everyone believes himself or herself to be an expert in everything. It has created a culture in which it is not okay to be wrong, in which we have convinced ourselves that our individual opinions are more valuable than facts determined through years of scientific study. Imagine her thoughts in 2021 as brave secondary educators all over the world attempt to prepare their students for a globalized world.

History of Experiential Learning

The historical foundations of experiential learning can be found in the philosophies of the three giants I've already mentioned; however, I would be remiss if the Association for Experiential Education (AEE) was not acknowledged.

The AEE has defined experiential learning "as a methodology in which educators direct students to a specific experience, and then guide the students through reflection to 'increase knowledge, develop skills, clarify values, and develop people's capacity to contribute to their communities'" (Behrendt & Franklin 2014, 237). At a conference in 1974, Henry Taft gave a speech titled "The Value of Experience" in which he said, "Finally I would hope that some sort of national organization on outdoor experiential education at the college level may evolve from this trailblazing meeting. You are in unexplored territory, and about to be impelled into experience. Good luck" (Taft, 1974).

In 1977, the Articles of Incorporation declared, "The stated purpose of this new association was to 'promote experiential education, support experiential educators, and further develop experiential learning" (Garvey 1995, 78). This style of education can aptly be placed firmly within the confines of the progressive education movement.

Outward Bound is another experiential learning organization, specializing in outdoor adventures. Both Outward Bound and the

AEE is that Outward Bound are adventure learning outfits, though the AEE exists within the education system as a method for educating future educators in the philosophy and methodology of this style of experiential learning. This methodology has gained traction over the years, though often with disadvantaged youth or students identified as being disciplinary problems within the traditional structure described in a previous chapter by Randolph S. Bourne.

Peter Allison and Kris Von Wald wrote in a study titled "Exploring values and personal and social development: learning through expeditions," published in 2010 in the journal *Pastoral Care in Education*, that international travel with some incorporation of outdoor education are believed by many to be crucial to the development of young people. The core argument the authors convey is that

> In order for such experiences to be of educational value we argue that creating space for students to make mistakes and to explore (in literal and metaphorical terms) is of crucial importance. The paper concludes that expeditions may provide a useful context for personal and social development and, in particular, exploration of values (Allison & Von Wald 2010, 219).

The literal space to explore is inherent in the outdoor segment of the experiential learning opportunity. What's not as clear is the metaphorical space to explore. At the secondary education level of global travel experiential learning opportunities, the metaphorical space to explore is provided by the reflective portion of the process following the experiential opportunity. Sir Ken Robinson says that schools kill creativity. If this is indeed true (and I think it is), then the moderate reformation that some speak of will not be adequate to address the issues. There needs to be radical change in education.

PART IV

Directions for Further Research

There are many avenues available for further research in this area. The first and most obvious avenue is to refine the current study so that it answers more questions that have a greater impact on the individual teacher. It would also be of benefit to have a greater pool of possible respondents. The study I undertook that led to this book is limited in scope in that regard. The original respondent pool was 210 and subsequently fell to 138 total respondents. Including schools on a national level would allow for real-world application of the results and findings.

Another avenue for further exploration within the context of this area of study would include gathering data on the relationship between socioeconomic status and participation in experiential learning opportunities. Because these opportunities often times come with a substantial price tag attached, it would be undeniably interesting to determine the impact of socioeconomic status on participation. The inclusion of socioeconomic status opens up so many interesting correlations. Couple that with a greater respondent pool and we have a study with serious real-world implications regarding the overall accessibility of these opportunities. I would argue that socioeconomic status is a great determiner of participation. Of course, many institutions with embedded experiential learning programs, such my workplace, have financial aid opportunities as well as scholarships.

It is my goal to carry on with a study that determines the impact of experiential learning on the transition from concrete to abstract thought within the stages of cognitive development. Does experiential learning make the transition from concrete to abstract thought faster? Does it play a role in speeding up the process of cognitive development from concrete to abstract thought? These are among the many questions that arise.

Over the course of the last two decades, experiential learning opportunities are becoming bolder and are expanding rapidly into secondary, middle, and lower schools across the nation.

I asked students to answer the question *In your own mind, what are the benefits of experiential learning?* All responses have been left completely unedited so as to retain their true feeling and meaning.

1. First hand experience with the world and you can find out more about yourself than you would find doing anything else.

2. It opened up my vision of the world. As an art student it allowed me to see what was in my textbooks, to experience such different culture and way of life was amazing. It changed me as a person. My focus for college changed because of my trip to France I want to pursue studies abroad and continue taking a language. International travel is an amazing opportunity and I am so glad I went. I learned things about myself, the world, French culture and custom, art and architecture, application of language etc . . .

3. In school we are told this is the right answer. We memorize it and understand the information but it is still just information. We forget most of the information we studied after the test. When we experience learning it sticks. We remember the entire learning experience for our entire lives, and will look back on it for the rest of our lives. It builds us into better people, a people

who has gained a unique experience that will shape the people we will become.

4. It gives the student an opportunity to experience and witness a different set of skills. In the classroom the learning experience is mostly about intellect and mental capabilities. When a student experience real life learning conditions it makes the student more aware and conscious of other aspects such as learning to read people and the situation and applying knowledge and information learned to real world experiences beyond just a test or exam.

5. The benefits are you get to see what it's like in a different culture and learn about it. You get to leave your comfort zone and try foods and things you might not do on your own. Traveling also gives you knowledge and understanding that books can't give you. It's something that when a teacher brings up in class a place, you can be like I've been there! It makes leaning so much more real and memorable.

6. The benefits of experiential learning are that a greater understanding of the world can be achieved than in a classroom setting. A traveler has the opportunity to put himself or herself in an unfamiliar position and setting which can allow them to grow as a person. Also, the people around the traveler can benefit as well through cultural or language exchange.

7. I believe experiential learning is a crucial part of the learning experience. Experiential learning provides students with a way to learn more about the world than can ever be learned in readings, lectures and daily classroom activities by allowing them to experience and serve on a firsthand basis. In the rest of my time at [school name], my goal is to take advantage of more [program name] trips because they have truly changed my life for the better.

8. The benefits are innumerable, I have learned that people of other parts of the world are just like us. There is a common language that all people share that has no words, and also that everybody can communicate through emotion. Travel for me, has broken down naïve barriers that I had formed in my conscience. I have a deeper understanding of humanity and what it means to be a person living in a global community. When people ask "why aren't you helping the people who need help in this community?" I now perceive my community to be the world's population. I think that experiential leaning has me subconsciously shaping my way of thinking.

I thought it best to conclude this section in part by letting the students speak for themselves regarding the benefits of experiential learning. What has become gospel for this author is that there are benefits to experiential learning that are unquantifiable—in fact, immeasurable. This truth makes it very difficult to prove any experiential learning program's worth to the educational community. We must keep in mind that there are benefits that cannot be measured—the greater sense of global awareness, the lifelong memories, the spiritual awakening—and they shouldn't be. Experiential learning can be a journey of intense personal worth, and this realm of benefit does not fall within the purview of ethical educational research. I leave you with one final response from a student that, frankly, is more profound than it first seems—"You can't get the experience any other way."

PART V

Conclusions and Solutions

E xperiential education, in nearly any capacity (though not all programs are created equally), is the key to creating a future of creative problem solvers, circular thinkers, and leaders who understand the connections between things. The system must be torn down and rebuilt from the ground up, taking into account the philosophical giants who were articulating problems with the industrial education system from its very inception.

The philosophical and intellectual changes addressed above are necessary structural changes. As for physical structural changes to the average secondary school, most seem to have been built on the premise of keeping students in—rather like prisons. This has an inherent negative psychological and neurological impact on the student as soon as they enter the building.

The physical structure, therefore, must more adequately address the psychological impact of closing students' minds prior to their arrival. Architects, working in concert with psychologists and neurologists, are creating incredibly stimulating environments that imbibe people with creativity and eagerness to engage. The school must be a relatively open space, while still addressing the very real security concerns of modern times.

What I am suggesting is a school with outdoor, open spaces in the interior, such as courtyards and atriums as well as glass walls and open doors. Further, the classroom itself must change. All classrooms should be part traditional space, part lab, and part art studio. Even the humanities classrooms must have space to create. Of course, there must be the lab space required for hand-on applications of the engineering, mathematical, architectural, and mechanical skills learned. This serves to embed the experience in the day. Not all experiences require traveling to the ends of the earth. These experiences do not all have to be cultural experiences. They can be embedded within the structure of the school day, provided the physical structure of the school is built to accommodate the types of classrooms needed.

Schools should be built to open the mind, to invite the mind to explore and develop the passions that set the soul on fire, not close it off upon entry. The space needs to be innovative and collaborative. The educators and students should be working in these spaces on various intellectually driven projects.

The educators should be working in concert with the students on various projects, nearly erasing the metaphorical line between them. This creates a more circular environment and a more inclusive community that begins to blur the dividing lines of the traditional classroom power structures.

Certainly, there are moments when educators must disseminate information, but this will be followed by practical applications of the material learned. There should be, built into the schedule, appropriate time given to the research endeavors of the educators themselves. That could include the specific content area of their teaching, or in specific pedagogies related to their craft. The idea would be to create a schedule that allows for both teachers and students to engage their passions and indeed work together on projects when those passions overlap.

The possibility of teams of students and teachers engaged in shared research projects is highly advised. This has to be left up to the professionalism of the educator, and the implementation of incredibly creative scheduling must coincide with these changes. This sounds like the functions of a university, but it should be implemented at the secondary level. The result will be earlier specialization, but that is not a negative, as some administrators in schools would have us believe. Many administrators believe that high school is meant to be a survey, but if you ask the students, they prefer to specialize. Through authentic relationships and experiences, students may be able to ascertain their specific interests at earlier stages in their development than previous generations. Of course, this is not for every student. As educators, we will still have to meet each student where they are.

The changes required are ultimately for the benefit of the student. They are changes that have been required since the industrialization and subsequent mass consumption of education, since long before Randolph S. Bourne wrote an essay outlining the problems with the industrialization of education in the November 17, 1914, issue of *The New Republic*. Mr. Bourne writes at length about the tedium of the classroom environment. It appears not much has changed. He wrote, "Is it not very curious that we spend so much time on the practice and methods of teaching, and never criticize the very framework itself? Call this thing that goes on in the modern schoolroom schooling if you like. Only don't call it education."

It's time to rethink how to engage students. The physical design of the classroom and building is as important as the intellectual design of the curriculum and its relationship to the authentic and integrated experiences provided within that curriculum by teachers.

It's time to criticize and tear down the old, tired framework. This is drastic yet necessary—in order to build a professional workforce of competent, analytical thinkers in the industries of the future, who are driven to arrive at data-backed solutions, and who are capable of problem-solving the most pressing issues of our time, building the human relationships necessary to enhance experiences like that of life aboard the *Bodrum*.

It is possible to accomplish this through an experiential model of education. The issue, as I see it, is that the divisiveness of our culture is created by a toxicity that has been sold to us like a casino sells a slot machine. This culture is reinforced by current stale systems of education in our country as well as curated social media accounts. We have to change the system to reinforce a new system of values, values that are entrenched in experiential models of education. Experiential education is the key to a brighter future. It has the potential to transform the way people think about the world and their home societies and cultures. It has the ability to give us back our souls. We're born, we work, and we die. It's no way to live.

Experiential education has the potential to change the way our students think about the world and subsequently have a positive impact on the way people all over the world view people in other parts of the world. It is imperative to include the triumvirate of experiential education which includes pre-curriculum, the experience itself, and proper reflection. We must be careful not to over-curricularize the programs, there must be room for experimentation within the context of the experience. Experiential education has the power to fundamentally create positive change in our world and our country through the simple act of taking off the blinders and allowing students to see the world as it really exists—not through the lens of a curated social media feed, virtual reality goggles, or virtual tours. Experiencing the smells, the sounds, the tastes, and the feel of a foreign culture are imperative to instilling understanding of other cultures. It has the power to eliminate the divisiveness of our society and has the potential to cure the boredom associated with the classical industrial-model classroom. Innovative spaces that provide room to create are imperative to the pre-curriculum, while personal space is required for proper and effective reflection. Rather than simply read about the Great Wall of China, why not build a scale replica? Rather than simply reading and calculating the requirements to construct a successful bridge, why not build one? Once this is complete, the students then visit the Great Wall or the Golden Gate Bridge or whatever the example may be. Upon return, proper written reflection must occur, during which the students engage with their experience after having lived it. What did they learn? How did they learn it? What aspect of the whole program was their favorite, and why? What would they change about their program, and why? Experiential education has the power to destroy the Western lines of divisiveness and create inclusive circles of thought that will be required for successful leadership in the future.

REFERENCES AND
FURTHER READING:

Allison, P. & Von Wald, K. "Exploring values and personal and social development: learning through expeditions." *Pastoral Care in Education,* 28, 219–233, 2010.

Aristotle. *Politics.* Translated by Benjamin Jowett. Chicago: William Benton, Publisher, 1952.

Batten, J. *Alone in the Sky.* United Kingdom: Airlife, 1979.

Beaudin, B.P. & Quick, D. "Experiential Learning: Theoretical Underpinnings." *HI-CAHS,* 1–25, 1995.

Behrendt, M & Franklin, T. "A Review of Research on School Field Trips and Their Value in Education." *International Journal of Environmental & Science Education,* 9, 235–245, 2014.

Bing, A.G. "Peace Studies as Experiential Education." *Annals of the American Academy of Social Sciences,* 504, 48–60, 1989.

Bourne, R. S. "In a Schoolroom." *The New Republic,* 1914.

Boyer, E. L. *College: The Undergraduate Experience in America.* New York, New York: Harper & Row, 1987.

Canadian Council on Learning. "The Impact of Experiential Learning Programs on Student Success." *Ontario Ministry of Education,* 1–54, 2009.

Cognetti, P. "Without Ever Reaching the Summit: A Journey." United States: Harper One.

The Complete I Ching. Translated by Taoist Master Alfred Huang. Rochester, VT: Inner Traditions, 2020.

Derrida, Jacques. *Writing and Difference*. Translated by Alan Bass. Chicago: The University of Chicago Press, 1978.

Descartes, Rene. *Rules for the Direction of the Mind*. Translated by Elizabeth S. Haldane and G.R.T. Ross. Chicago: William Benton, Publisher, 1952.

Descartes, Rene. *Discourse on the Method of Rightly Conducting the Reason*. Translated by Elizabeth S. Haldane and G.R.T. Ross. Chicago: William Benton, Publisher, 1952.

Descartes, Rene. *Meditations on First Philosophy*. Translated by Elizabeth S. Haldane and G.R.T. Ross. Chicago: William Benton, Publisher, 1952.

Descartes, Rene. *Objections Against the Meditations, and Replies*. Translated by Elizabeth S. Haldane and G.R.T. Ross. Chicago: William Benton, Publisher, 1952.

Dewey, J. *Experience & Education*. New York, New York: Simon & Schuster, 1938.

Engels, F., Marx, K. The Communist Manifesto. United States: Knopf Doubleday Publishing Group, 2019.

Garvey, D. A History of AEE. In Warren, K., Sakofs, M., Hunt, J.S. (Eds.), *The Theory of Experiential Education*. 75–83. Boulder, CO: Kendall/Hunt Publishing Company, 1995.

Hansen, E. *Stranger in the Forest: On Foot Across Borneo*. United States: Vintage Books, 2000.

Holtzman, R. "Experiential Learning in Washington, D.C.: A Study of Student Motivations and Expectations." *Transformative Dialogues: Teaching and Learning Journal.* 5, 1–11, 2011.

Kerins, A.T. *An Adventure in Service Learning: Developing Knowledge, Values and Responsibility.* Surrey, England: Gower Publishing Limited, 2010.

Klika, S.C. The Value of Travel. *American School Board Journal.* 33–34, 2008.

Kolb, D.A. *Experiential Learning: Experience as the Source of Learning and Development.* Englewood Cliffs, NJ: Prentice Hall, Inc., 1984.

Kozol, J. *Savage Inequalities: Children in America's Schools.* New York, NewYork: Harper Perennial, 1992.

Laborde, D., Bizikova, L., Lallemant, T., & Smaller, C. (Rep.). International Institute for Sustainable Development (IISD). Retrieved from http://www.jstor.org/stable/resrep17133, 2016.

Lao Tzu. *Tao Te Ching.* Translated and Annotated by Derek Lin. Nashville, TN: Skylight Paths Publishing, 2015.

Liberman, Kenneth "Decentering the Self: Two Perspectives from Philosophical Anthropology," in Dallery, A.B. and Scott, C.E. (eds.) *The Question of the Other: Essays in Contemporary Continental Philosophy.* Albany: State University of New York Press, pp. 127–142, 1989.

Locke, John *Concerning Civil Government, Second Essay.* Chicago: William Benton, Publisher, 1952.

Locke, John *Second Treatise of Government.* in Classics of Moral and Political Theory. Edited by Michael M. Morgan. Cambridge: Hackett Publishing Company, 1996.

Mead, L.A. Value of Foreign Travel. *The Journal of Education.* 108 (18), 464–465, 1928.

Miettinen, R. "The concept of experiential learning and John Dewey's theory of reflective thought and action." *International Journal of Lifelong Education.* 19, 54–72, 2000.

Piaget, J. *Genetic Epistemology.* W.W. Norton & Company, 1970.

Plato *Apology.* in Classics of Moral and Political Theory. Edited by Michael M. Morgan. Cambridge: Hackett Publishing Company, 1996.

Plato *Crito.* Translated by Benjamin Jowett. Chicago: William Benton, Publisher, 1952.

Plato *Gorgias.* Translated by Benjamin Jowett. Chicago: William Benton, Publisher, 1952.

Plato *Laws.* Translated by Benjamin Jowett. Chicago: William Benton, Publisher, 1952.

Plato *Republic.* Translated by Benjamin Jowett. Chicago: William Benton, Publisher, 1952.

Roberts, L.P. & Moon, R.A. "Community Service Learning Methodology and Academic Growth in Secondary School Content Disciplines: An Action-Research Study." *High School Journal.* 80, 1–6, 1997.

Robinson, Sir Ken. *Out of Our Minds: Learning to be Creative.* Westford, MA: Capstone Publishing Ltd., 2011.

Robinson, Sir Ken. *The Element: How Finding Your Passion Changes Everything.* Penguin Books, 2010.

Rousseau, Jean Jacques *Social Contract.* Translated by G. D. H. Cole. Chicago: William Benton, Publisher, 1952.

Salter, C.A. & Teger, A.I. Change in Attitudes Toward Other Nations as a Function of the Type of International Contact. *Sociometry.* 38, 213–222, 1975.

Spinoza, Baruch *Ethics.* Translated by W.H. White, Revised by A.H. Sterling. Chicago: William Benton, Publisher, 1952.

Stoner, K.R., Tarrant, M.A., Perry, L., Stoner, L., Wearing, S., Lyons, K., "Global Citizenship as a Learning Outcome of Educational Travel." *Journal of Teaching in Travel and Tourism.* 14, 149–163, 2013.

Synnott, M. "The Impossible Climb: Alex Honnold, El Capitan, and the Climbing Life." United States: Penguin Publishing Group, 2020.

Tarrant, M. & Lyons, K. The effect of short-term educational travel programs on environmental citizenship. *Environmental Education Research.* 18, 403–416, 2012.

Web pages

· ·

The United Nations Educational, Scientific and Cultural Organization, UNESCO, www.unesco.org

Data about the United States education system, www.educationdata.org

The International Institute for Sustainable Development, www.iisd.org

The Association for Experiential Education, www.aee.org

The National Society for Experiential Education, www.nsee.org

Global Education Benchmark Group, www.gebg.org

Outward Bound, www.outwardboung.org

College Board, www.collegeboard.org

TRACC, www.tracc.org

Tunku Putra International School, www.tphs.edu.my

APPENDIX A

A Note on the Reflection Process

According to the Association for Experiential Learning, "Experiential learning occurs when carefully chosen experiences are supported by reflection, critical analysis and synthesis."

It is well known in experiential learning circles that including adequate time for appropriate preparation and reflection on the experience is a necessary component of the post-experience period as well as during the experience. Many times, experiential learning in secondary schools misses this mark. The reason being that the program experience takes place during the first few weeks of summer. This means as soon as the students get back, they are out of the educator's hands and are therefore left to their own devices to reflect. While I am an advocate for fewer curricularized experiences, the reflection is one aspect that requires some guidance. This will work for some students, but others need guided reflection in the form of specific questions to help them process how they felt about their own experience. It is also important to understand that reflection does not have to be written; students are still guaranteed choice. Of course, it could be an essay, but it could also be a photography portfolio, a presentation, a piece of artwork, or a piece of music. In the pages that follow, I offer a space for reflection for all readers, not just students. I offer guided questions below in order to start the thinking process, but your reflection is yours.

Questions to consider for your own further reflection:

1. What assumptions or expectations did you bring to the experience? To what extent were they accurate?

2. What values, opinions, and beliefs have changed for you?

3. What is something you learned that you didn't think you would? What surprised you?

4. What did you learn about yourself? Did this experience change you in any way? If so, how?

5. Would you do this again? Why or why not? What would you change about the experience, positive or negative?

6. What were the most difficult parts of this experience? Why?

7. What were the most satisfying parts of the experience? Why?

8. How did this experience challenge you?

9. In which moments did you feel disconnected and disengaged? Why?

10. In which moments did you feel connected and engaged? Why?

11. What are some other ideas for future projects, designs, or experiences? [1,2]

---

1   Adapted from The DEAL Model developed by Dr. Patti Clayton and Sarah ASH http://curricularengagement.com/handouts/ http://servicelearning.duke.edu/up-loads/media_items/deal-reflection-questions.original.pdf

2   Produced by the Experiential Learning Office, Ryerson University, 2009 chrome-extension://efaidnbmnnnibpcajpcglclefindmkaj/viewer.html?pdfurl=https%3A%2F%2Fwww.mcgill.ca%2Feln%2Ffiles%2Feln%2Fdoc_ryerson_criticalreflection.pdf&clen=449949&chunk=true

REFLECTIONS:

CPSIA information can be obtained
at www.ICGtesting.com
Printed in the USA
JSHW020147130622
26816JS00005B/162